NEGOTIATING WITH YOUR EX

Divorce Is Only the Beginning

rh

NEGOTIATING WITH YOUR EX

Divorce Is Only the Beginning

Brad McRae

Self-Counsel Press
(a division of)
International Self-Counsel Press Ltd.
USA   Canada

Self-Counsel Press acknowledges the financial support of the Government of Canada through the Canada Book Fund (CBF) for our publishing activities.

Printed in Canada.

First edition: 2015

Library and Archives Canada Cataloguing in Publication

McRae, Bradley C. (Bradley Collins), 1945-, author
    Negotiate with your ex : divorce is only the beginning / Brad McRae.

(Legal series)
Issued in print and electronic formats.
ISBN 978-1-77040-224-9 (pbk.).—ISBN 978-1-77040-984-2 (epub).—ISBN 978-1-77040-985-9 (kindle)

    1. Divorce. 2. Interpersonal conflict. 3. Negotiation. I. Title.
II. Series: Self-Counsel legal series

HQ814.M385 2015   306.89   C2014-908247-9
                                                    C2014-908248-7

Self-Counsel Press
(a division of)
International Self-Counsel Press Ltd.

Bellingham, WA   North Vancouver, BC
USA   Canada

Contents

3 Develop a Negotiating Plan

4 Understand the Stages

5 Make Your Negotiating Style Work for You, Not Against You

8 How to Negotiate with a Difficult Ex-Spouse 129

9 Seek Mediation 159

10 Forgive Yourself and Your Ex-Spouse 185

Conclusion 199

Download Kit 203

Exercises

Samples

Tables

Notice to Readers

Laws are constantly changing. Every effort is made to keep this publication as current as possible. However, the author, the publisher, and the vendor of this book make no representations or warranties regarding the outcome or the use to which the information in this book is put and are not assuming any liability for any claims, losses, or damages arising out of the use of this book. The reader should not rely on the author or the publisher of this book for any professional advice. Please be sure that you have the most recent edition.

Although the skills, strategies and techniques that are documented in this book will work in a number of situations, there is no guarantee that they will work in your particular case. Therefore, if you continue to have difficulty negotiating with your ex-spouse, I recommend that you seek qualified professional help.

Dedication

Going through a separation and divorce, especially when there are children involved, can be one of the most difficult transitions we ever have to face, and in many cases it may feel like we have to face this transition alone. Unlike marriage, or the birth of a child, there is none of the usual forms of social support. Many of our friends, especially friends of both parties, feel awkward in supporting one party or the other, and end up supporting neither. Or the support is there initially, but few people realize the time necessary to make the complete transition. There are, however, special people (angels) who seem to come out of the woodwork and lend their support through these difficult times. It is to those people who instantly know the right thing to do or say and support us and help us heal that this book is dedicated.

In that respect, I would like to dedicate this book to our nanny, Marilyn Christie; to John Loback, Terrye Perlman, Carla Angleheart, and Michele Vyge-Fraser, for supporting us; to the Findlays who invited us to countless fun activities; and to my two wonderful children, Andrew Collins McRae and Kathryn Crosby McRae, who delight in providing additional lessons on the road to lifelong learning.

Acknowledgments

There are many people I would like to thank for their help and support in the writing of this book. My sincere thanks to all of the people I interviewed for this book; although their identities have been changed, they will recognize their own stories. Each of these kind and brave souls added significantly to my understanding of the problems, challenges, and concerns that people going through this process have to cope with and what they learned in the process, and for their willingness to share those hard-earned lessons with the rest of us.

I would also like to acknowledge the following people, without whose help and support this book could not have been written: Katherine Coy, Joan Homewood, Marilyn Christie, and Lawrence McEachern, my home editing team. Last, I would like to thank my support team: my two wonderful children, Andrew and Kathryn McRae, and my best friends, Terrye Perlman, Carla Angleheart, Michele Vyge-Fraser, Rita Wuebbeler, and John Loback.

Preface

There has been far too much debate about whether the children of divorced parents are better off if the parents divorce than they would be if the parents stay together for the sake of the children, and not enough information on how former spouses can negotiate to make the new reality work. Go into any bookstore and you will find hundreds of books on relationships. You will be lucky if you find one or two helpful books on divorce and separation. In the last sentence I chose the word "helpful" with care because there are some books that are written in this area that make former spouses feel guilty rather than help them. *Negotiating with Your Ex* has been written to fill that void.

Skill development in negotiating and influencing is much like parenting. Our parenting skills have to change and adapt as we and our children grow older. The skills that work perfectly well with a 6-year-old will not work at all with a 16-year-old. Using the same line of reasoning, the skills you developed that worked when you were a married couple may no longer work now that you are separated and/or divorced.

I have been studying the negotiation process for over 30 years. I am the author of *Negotiating and Influencing Skills: The Art of Creating and Claiming Value*, *The Seven Strategies of Master Negotiators* and publisher and editor of *The Negotiation Newsletter*. Until the time of my own divorce, most of my time was spent looking at negotiating and influencing skills in business and organizational settings. As I progressed through my divorce, I found that although there were many excellent resources available to help get through divorce or separation, there were not many resources to help once you get through a divorce, especially if there were children involved. In cases where there are children involved, most ex-spouses are horrified when they learn that instead of negotiating less frequently, they find that they have to negotiate more frequently. So 10 years after my divorce, I started to write *Negotiating with Your Ex*. It is based on my own experience as a divorced father, the experiences of the 78 people I interviewed for the book, and from the best literature on how to negotiate effectively.

Introduction: Are You a Victim, Survivor, or Thriver?

When I read the letter from his lawyer, I knew instantly that I was getting the short end of the stick. This official document was the first indication that the relationship was over. Intellectually, I understood the words on the page yet the message was surreal. Instinctively, my guard was up and I sensed that the timing of this news had been carefully planned in advance. Emotionally, the shock factor kept me from doing any physical damage to either of us or the house.

He packed. He left.

I stayed. Paced. Sorted. Emailed friends for insight. Tried to find my spirit. That was the first six hours. At 8:00 a.m., the phone rang. A trusted friend and colleague, who is a strategic planner, shook me out of the emotional drama and thrust me into the foray of negotiating. With a tone fit for her staff in Washington, DC, she advised me that this was the ultimate moment to plan, and we would start now.

"Just the facts," she said.

We created a list. It kept me busy for the day. I pulled documents from drawers, wrote phone numbers and contacts for lawyers, accountants, and other professionals.

My anger created the energy I needed to start my engines and take control.

The first 24 hours were more productive than most business days, with a heavy agenda. My focus was diverted from sinking into an emotional abyss and getting even, to figuring out what to do and how to do it. The next 24 hours — and I don't deny or trivialize the emotions — involved searching for his motivation to call off our 20-year relationship so unexpectedly.

Again and again, I went over my memories, and my newly formed suspicions, as I tried to sort out the facts from my imagination.

Finally, on day four, I carefully chose my lawyer. I explained that I wanted to develop the contractual agreements and negotiate with my ex personally. I also said that I did need legal advice and expertise, so that I did not inadvertently put myself at risk, and I asked my lawyer how we could work together to minimize my expenses.

My ex and I began the negotiations two weeks later. My goal was to establish the setting that would create and maintain maximum value for both of us. I suggested that we make a list to divide the property and prioritize our wants. I kept my options open, neither denying nor agreeing that he should buy me out — requiring me to move out of the house, and also relocate my business — as his lawyer had demanded. I knew that I would prefer not to let go of the property, but he did not need to have that information at this point. We signed and dated our first draft agreement; he generously wrote a check to purchase my share of our recreational belongings. That's where his interests and needs were satisfied. This initial exercise also confirmed for me that his negotiation style was competitive, where mine was cooperative. I posted the chart describing the difference in styles on my fridge, ready to deal effectively with the next ultimatum.

All in all, the negotiation spanned two years. My long-held belief, that timing is important in sports and in life, helped me to manage the negotiation process. In the meanwhile, my ex found a new bride; his financial situation put extra pressure on him, as did his family who wanted him to move on and "get this over with."

The strategic alliances with my lawyer, my colleagues, and my friends helped me to stay on track. The cycle of negotiations was repeated often before the final transaction was made. During this time, I captured all of our discussions meticulously on paper, so that when threats were made, I had factual proof of the decisions we had made together. Some meetings were painful; others very businesslike. We both dated and initialed all decisions and kept copies for reference. The notes became the basis for the final contractual document, which included the transfer of the deed for the house and property. My lawyer made sure that we had covered all the potential loopholes, and then stamped the contract with his official seal of approval. When the package was delivered to my ex, with [my] bank check for the buyout [of the house], I was not surprised to have it rejected.

The lawyer representing my ex again coerced him into thinking that he could get more if there were limitations set to the transfer of the property. She appealed to his competitive style. Over the phone, I clearly kept to the process I had established stating five factual objections to his counteroffer, to which I would need his lawyer's legal responses. This stopped him in his tracks. It was obvious that only one negotiator's wallet would be emptied by this maneuver. My ex signed that day.

True to the original plan, I did not exceed the maximum retainer target for my legal advisor. In fact, my deed to the property was accompanied by a rebate check from my lawyer for 25 percent of the original retainer. My lawyer telephoned that same day to say, "You're one of the best negotiators I've had as a client." I learned that it is a process of learning to push forward and pull back, all the while staying incredibly patient, alert, and focused on a flexible end result.

Eve (all of the names of the people I interviewed for the book have been changed to ensure their anonymity) may not have realized it, but she was not alone. There are over 26 million people who are separated or divorced in North America and there are two million additional couples in the process of becoming separated or divorced every year. Eve also may not have realized that she had a vital decision to make as she went through the process of becoming separated and divorced, and that decision was whether to be a victim, a survivor, or a thriver.

1. Victims, Survivors, and Thrivers

All people going through a divorce or any traumatic experience can be categorized into one of three groups:

- Victims.

- Survivors.

- Thrivers.

When facing a divorce or separation, some people become victims of the process. For example, when I interviewed Ted, he said that, in retrospect, he put his life and his family's life on hold for years. There were drawn-out legal battles, escalating costs, and an inability to enjoy himself as well as his children, because all of his focus had been on winning the legal battle with his ex-wife. As a result, his whole family became victimized by the process. Other victims never fully recover emotionally and become stuck in the past — often blaming their ex-spouses for their inability to recover.

The second choice we can make is to become a survivor. Most people survive by doing the best they can under the circumstance. When all is said and done, survivors do all right, but their futures are never as good as they could or should be. Although surviving is a much better choice than being a victim, thriving is better than surviving. Thrivers know that change is also an opportunity for growth. Sometimes looking for that opportunity is like looking for the proverbial needle in a haystack. But if you look hard enough — it is there.

One of my favorite examples of thrivers is the story of James and Elizabeth. During our interview, James said:

> When it became abundantly clear that we couldn't save our marriage, we decided to separate. It was without a doubt the most difficult decision either of us ever had to make because family is so important to us and we were devastated that we could not provide that for our three children. At the same time, we did not want to model staying together for the sake of the children because we did not want them to learn that it was OK to stay in a relationship that was not good for them. The other significant issue, of course, was money. As it was, we were just making ends meet to be able to afford one house so there was no way we could afford two houses or even one house and an apartment after we separated.

Elizabeth said:

> I told James that it wasn't a house that gave us or our children a sense of home and community. I reminded him that some of our happiest times were when we lived in a basement apartment after we were first married. Then I suggested that if we could find two reasonably priced apartments, so that our children could continue to go to school with the children that they had always gone to school with, play sports with the children that they had always played sports with, and stay involved in most of the extracurricular activities that they had been involved with, we could keep their sense of community almost totally intact. I also told him that it would not diminish my sense of James as a provider because I knew that was so important to his sense of self.

James said:

> At first, I just couldn't stand the thought of our children no longer living in a house. But after Elizabeth spoke so eloquently about working to preserve our children's sense of community, I felt that there was something that I, and we, could do that was positive for our children. Three years later, I even found that living in an apartment had certain advantages. All of the time that I used to spend maintaining the house, I now spend doing activities with the children so that I actually spend a lot more time with them and am a better father than I was before.

Thrivers eventually use their separations and/or divorces as growth experiences and learn how to have happier, healthier, and more fulfilled lives. As thrivers, James and Elizabeth discovered focus management. Focus management is actively looking for and focusing on those positive things that one can do and have control over rather than focusing on the things that you can't do or don't have control over. There are times when we can take more active control over our circumstances than we think. We just need a mental model to help us to see how.

Becoming a thriver is not an easy process, but if you follow the strategies that are described in this book, you will see that it can be done. Therefore, from the individuals and couples I interviewed, from reading the literature on separation and divorce and on negotiating skills and strategies, I will present the most effective mental models and strategies that you can use so that you can negotiate as effectively as possible with your ex-spouse or ex-partner. (For the purposes of this book, the terms ex-spouse and ex-partner will be used synonymously.)

That said, there is no question that separating and divorcing is often one of life's most difficult transitions. The negotiations, both during and after the separation and/or divorce, are often hard fought, emotionally draining, and the process is often non-stop — because even when you think you have finished negotiating, at least for the time being, there are often unanticipated and messy details that arise that throw you right back into the negotiation process. At the same time, you are often angry and emotionally exhausted. Everything in your life seems different and there are a million things that need to be accomplished to the point where it feels like your life is one difficult negotiation after another, and the process seems and sometimes is never ending. For example, if there are children, there is a never ending series of negotiations from who gets to buy that most requested extra special Christmas present, to how clean is clean for their rooms, to what is a reasonable time to come home for teenagers, to how each ex-spouse should pay to help out with expenses for post-secondary education or a child's wedding, to how much time you get to spend with your grandchildren after your children have children.

However, negotiating well will not only help at the time, it will also set important precedents that can help with future negotiations, and help you become good role models in how to deal effectively with differences if there are children involved. In fact, if done correctly, you can survive and even thrive if you learn how to negotiate through the emotional and psychological turbulence inherent in the process.

People who courageously managed this transition, rather than having the transition manage them, will tell their stories throughout this book. You will also have an opportunity to learn from cases where the parties negotiated poorly and learn that there are viable alternatives that you can use when negotiation is not the best way for the parties to come to agreement. Some of the examples that will be used in the book take place in the early stages of separating, like Eve's story, however, most of the examples focus on the ongoing negotiations that ex-spouses must face.

Unlike a marriage, during a divorce or separation there is often little social support. Instead of friends coming together for a celebration, friends are busy choosing or being forced to choose sides, or are afraid of not maintaining their neutrality and end up supporting neither ex-spouse. When people marry, there are often socially supportive events such as bachelor and bachelorette parties, and bridal showers. However, there are few forms of social support for divorcing and separating couples. It is difficult for all involved: ex-spouses, children, grandparents, relatives and friends. It is also difficult for the children's friends. Everyone is reacting to the divorce and/or separation in different ways and all of this is happening at the same time. Add to this a society that still remains, at best, not supportive of people going through this process. At its worst, the message you receive is that you have failed in your own marriage, you will be doomed to fail in any future relationship, and you are dooming your children to a life of not being able to have or maintain any type of long-term relationship, and/or that your children now come from a broken home — all of which is not true.

Many people have made this transition successfully and so can you. It is also true that the transition is often much more difficult if there are children involved who are living at home, because as most divorcing and separating couples with children soon find out, they have to negotiate more frequently after the divorce and/or separation than they ever had to do before.

In all negotiations, there are two important factors to keep in mind. First, as difficult as it is to negotiate effectively, it is often more difficult to know when to negotiate and when not to negotiate. As Shakespeare said, "Ripeness is all," which means timing is everything, that is we must determine to the best of our abilities when to and when not to bring up issues. Secondly, it is equally important to note that every negotiation sets either a positive or a negative precedent for all subsequent negotiations. The following story illustrates each of these crucial points.

> When Chris and Allie separated, it looked like it would be a battle royale over who had custody of their young son and daughter. Allie's original position was that the children would live with her and Chris would have the children one night a week and every other weekend. Chris' original position was that they would each have the children half of the time. However, it wasn't until Chris and Allie's lawyers looked behind each party's position and came up with a creative solution that the two parties were able to agree.
>
> Allie wanted stability, and to her that meant that the children should spend as much time with her as possible. Chris was deeply involved in his children's lives and could not stand the thought of being a "once a week and every other weekend" dad. The final plan that they agreed

upon was that Allie's apartment would be the primary residence. Chris would have the children every second weekend, but those would be extended weekends starting Thursday night and ending Monday morning, when the children were dropped off at daycare and preschool. On the weekends when Allie had the children, Chris would have the children for two nights during the week. Although it took some time to hammer out this arrangement, both Allie and Chris felt that it was workable for them and their children.

When there are children, deciding on a shared parenting agreement is often the most difficult negotiation. Please note I use the words "shared parenting agreement" in place of the word "custody." The problem with the word "custody" is that by its very nature it is adversarial — the children are either with one parent or the other. The words "shared parenting agreement" imply that there is more than enough parenting available to both parents if a creative enough arrangement can be worked out. Those first separation or post-divorce negotiations set viable or unviable precedents for all of the negotiations that will follow. The following story illustrates just how long the negotiation process can last.

We separated when my daughter Jane was eight, and we are still negotiating, although not nearly as frequently, 20 years later. Jane is getting married in eight months so we had to sit down and plan the wedding and work out the hundreds of details, such as who is responsible for what and who pays for what.

At first my ex-wife, Martha, did not want to sit down with me. However, both Jane and I told her that it was eight months away and that we all had a common interest in making it the best wedding possible for Jane. Martha said that she would work with us on the condition that my current wife not attend the wedding. (I am not advocating this as a solution. However, it was the solution that was agreed to in this particular situation.) It was agreed to reluctantly and then everything worked out rather well. We decided that Martha would pay for the wedding dress, the bridesmaid's dresses, the flowers, and the brunch for the wedding party. I would be responsible for the reception, and the two amounts were approximately equal.

As you can see from these stories, every negotiation has a life of its own, and each negotiation will set the tone for future negotiations.

Therefore, wise ex-spouses will set that tone very carefully because no one ever knows what joys and tragedies the future has in store for us. The fact that Martha and Simon were able to come together for the sake of their daughter's wedding makes it more likely that they will be able to negotiate other issues in the future.

2. Negotiating with an Ex-Spouse Who Is Negotiating in Bad Faith

Although this book focuses on how to negotiate positively with your ex-spouse, it would be naïve to assume that all negotiations can turn out positively. Therefore, it is just as important to know how to make a wise decision when you are better off not negotiating as the following examples point out.

> When Keith and Betty decided to separate, their agreement was that Keith would find an apartment and move out. In the meantime, their house would be put up for sale, the proceeds from the house would be split equally, and Betty would buy her own place.
>
> They still had one child living at home, 17-year-old Sam. At the time, Sam was a poor student, was addicted to alcohol and marijuana, and was in the process of amassing a criminal record to support his addictions.
>
> Keith informed Betty and Sam that he had rented a one-bedroom apartment and therefore he would only be able to take Sam on selected weekends, because, after all, he only had one bedroom. In other words, Keith had decided, unilaterally, that Betty would be responsible for most, if not all, of the childrearing.
>
> Even if this were the best solution, the process stunk. First, Keith left Betty with little if any input into the childrearing arrangements. The psychological message to Sam was loud and clear: his father did not want him. Keith also tried to put Betty into a double bind. If she brought the issue up, Keith would label her behavior as nagging. If she didn't bring it up, she felt taken advantage of and resentful of the way Keith treated her and Sam.
>
> In the end, Betty wrote Keith a letter explaining her thoughts and feelings. She then told Sam that she would help him conquer his addictions, deal with his legal problems, and help him graduate from high school. She set

down some firm guidelines that Sam would have to obey if he were to live in her house. She also decided, that regardless of how unfair the process was, it would be better for Sam to be in one place where he received consistent support and that Keith's behavior was tangible proof that her marriage to Keith couldn't work and that Keith had shown his true colors both to Betty and Sam.

In this case, Betty realized that the negotiation was not between Betty and Keith, because she could not trust that Keith could or would negotiate in good faith. Betty rightly recognized that this negotiation was firstly a negotiation between Betty and herself, internally, about acknowledging Keith's lack of respect for both herself and their son. Second, Betty recognized that she could do nothing other than recognize Keith's behavior of negotiating in bad faith. Third, Keith was not likely to change, and fourth, that Betty now had an opportunity to negotiate more consistently with Sam about what was, and what was not, acceptable behavior in her house. Last, Betty hired a lawyer and was successful in recovering monetary support from Keith until Sam graduated from high school.

There are a number of people who just plain refuse to negotiate, or who have personality disorders, borderline personalities, narcissistic personalities, or addictions. Sometimes, you must limit the number of negotiations or interactions or stop negotiating or interacting all together. An example is Estelle's story.

I asked my former husband to stop calling altogether last spring. He had been working in New York and when he was feeling lonely, he would drink. He would then phone the kids and try to speak with them while drunk. This made them extremely uncomfortable and I put a stop to it as soon as I could. I didn't ask my kids if I should do this; I felt I had to protect them so I just acted and explained later. He hasn't contacted them since. I should probably add that three years ago when our son Zach was diagnosed with cancer and went through a year of chemotherapy, I asked their father to write to the boys once a week to cheer them up. He couldn't even manage that so I felt no sympathy for him when he was needy.

Likewise, Cindy left her physically abusive husband, Hal, when her children were eight months and two-and-a-half years old. When I asked her to describe the situation, she said:

As you might imagine I felt very torn about his having on-going contact with the children. On the one hand, he was the children's father and I wanted them to have at least some sense of the man who was their biological father, in particular and what the role of a father is, in general, especially since they were both boys. I also felt that it was important for the children to know their roots on their father's side of the family in addition to their mother's because that is such an important part of who they are. On the other hand, I did not want my boys to be subjected to a man who was physically abusive to their mother, was an alcoholic, and couldn't get his act together. In a way, I think I was lucky because we were living in Europe at the time, so moving back to North America put some distance between the children and me, and their father. As a result, he has had little contact with us.

I didn't say very much to the children about their father for the first years, because I didn't feel that I could be objective. I was too angry, hurt and betrayed. I was also feeling caught between wanting them to know the truth and in wanting to protect my children from the truth. I also guess I was hoping he would get his act together. In the end I encouraged communication with ways they could speak regularly and with the occasional visit. For the first few years he was interested in being part of their lives and he did make some of the maintenance payments. Then the contact became less and less.

I always did my best to build their beliefs about healthy relationships. As they got older, I told them more about what happened and that there are times in any relationship where you have to draw the line around what is appropriate behavior and what is not. I also told them that their relationship with their father was different from mine and that I wanted them to evaluate the situation for themselves and make up their own minds.

The hardest time for them was Father's Day at school, when the kids were given time in class to make Father's Day gifts and my children didn't have a father who was part of their lives to make gifts for. I decided to get them a Big Brother who became a friend of the family and spent some real quality time with the boys.

I also discovered that some boys need men in their lives more than others. I noticed that my youngest son was particularly attentive and sometimes clingy when my brothers or other men that he liked came over to the house. Because our society is still so nuclear family oriented — just watch the shows or ads on TV — I think not having a father around left a big hole in their lives, so I worked really hard to make sure they knew they were loved by me. It also helped that many of my children's friends are from divorced homes.

Cindy's story is a great example of acceptance and giving herself time to integrate this experience into her life. She also demonstrated a great sense of self-control and timing in deciding not to talk to her children about their father when she first separated as she realized she could not be objective.

From all of the interviews, one of the most striking observations I made was the positive power of constructive precedents and the negative power of harmful precedents. For example, there have been many cases where the child has been given too much power; for example, a child who decides to live exclusively with one parent, that is, "the good parent," and not spend any time living with "the bad parent." That precedent has come back to haunt them when the child then decides that the good parent is really the bad parent and vice versa.

Eileen and her new husband, Lawrence, had decided that they wanted a new start. They did not like the racial politics that pervaded their African homeland, and were successful in their application to immigrate to North America. Lawrence's children were grown, but Eileen had a 15-year-old son, David. As Eileen had primary custody, this meant that David would also move to North America. However, after three months of total unhappiness, David decided that he would move back to Africa and live with his Dad. Eileen was devastated. She couldn't stand for David to be so far away, nor could she stand to see her son so homesick and unhappy.

This was not the first time, nor will it be the last, when parents have moved children away from the other parent, or one of the parents has moved out of state or province to find a better job, only to realize that they had to move back, or risk having very little time with their child or children. In other words, this type of decision must be made carefully.

Another example where the process worked out poorly for all of the parties involved is the story of Joe and Ann.

Joe and Ann had had a stormy relationship beginning in the second year of their marriage. They had one child, Frank. When they separated, Frank decided that he wanted to live with his father because he found his mother to be too strict. Several years later, Joe remarried. Frank became heavily involved with an addictive computer game. By this time Frank was spending 40 hours a week on the game and the game had become more important to Frank than his schoolwork, his friends, and his family. Frank subsequently moved in with his mother because she now appeared to be the least strict of his two parents.

Unfortunately, Frank never learned how to negotiate his differences with either parent, and was able to play one parent off against the other. To make matters worse, Frank's writing off one parent or the other at various times, left the parent who has been written off feeling betrayed, invalidated, and disenfranchised. For the first two years of their separation, Frank had very little contact with his mother. Now he has no contact with his father.

In those cases where the parties can negotiate and sincerely want to engage in side-by-side problem-solving rather than confrontation, an excellent way to proceed in their current and future negotiations is to learn to use the strategies and skills that are illustrated in the ten chapters of this book. Although this book emphasizes how to negotiate as effectively as possible, we have to recognize that sometimes things simply cannot be changed or the massive amount of effort to change them results in few, if any, positive results. Therefore, one of the hardest things to learn as a negotiator is when to negotiate and when not to negotiate, and it takes a lot of wisdom to know the difference. One of my favorite stories on how difficult wisdom is to attain follows.

A woman who was travelling in Tibet came across a cemetery. Upon closer inspection, the woman was shocked to see how short the lifespan was of the people who were buried there: one year, two years, three and a quarter years, etc. She thought that a terrible epidemic must have caused so much pain and suffering among the children of the village. On the way out, she saw an old Buddhist priest and decided to ask him about the terrible misfortune that had come to the village. The priest reflected and then his face broke into a beaming smile. He then said, "I am sorry but you must have misunderstood. This is a Buddhist cemetery and we only measure the number of enlightened years that a person has lived."

It is my hope that the stories and research in this book will help you take a more enlightened approach to what can be one of life's most difficult transitions. By using the 10 strategies described in this book, you will be able to make better decisions on how to negotiate and make wiser decisions on when to and when not to negotiate. To begin this journey, we must learn to build the future with creative solutions.

1

Build Your Future with Creative Solutions

There is a plethora of creative solutions to help separated and divorced couples; however, for the most part, these creative solutions reside only in the hands of the people who made them and/or their immediate circles of friends and relatives. The goal of this book is to illustrate as many creative solutions as possible in one place so that divorcing or separating individuals do not have to reinvent the wheel, and to give them the tools they need to develop their own innovative solutions. The numerous examples in this chapter will:

1. Help you develop a greater appreciation of the options that exist.

2. Help you to learn how to more effectively develop your own creative solutions tailored to your specific needs.

Please note that most of the examples that follow relate to creative housing/living arrangements. This was done to help the reader get a sense of the variety of creative solutions that exist. The other chapters in this book deal with many of the other issues that need to be negotiated.

When Ingrid and Keith separated, Ingrid and their two daughters lived in the matrimonial house for the first year and Keith lived in a small bachelor apartment. Both reported that this arrangement was extremely difficult financially because it left little disposable income for anything else. They also reported that it was difficult psychologically:

Keith felt that he was missing out on his children's lives and Ingrid felt that she was hostage to taking care of the house and the children. The couple knew they would have to sell the matrimonial home and considered several options after that.

Ingrid reported that:

> We thought that a set of flats in the same building was preferable because we wanted to remain in our neighborhood and we couldn't afford the matrimonial home and an apartment although we tried it for the first year. Plus the children were young and it was a lot of work taking them with me every time I needed something at the store and it was impractical to get a sitter. So by the end of the first year, I was pretty exhausted. At first, Keith wasn't comfortable with the idea of flats, but once I showed him my reasoning and gave him some time to come around, he agreed to give it a try. We decided that we would try it for a year and renew on a yearly basis only if everyone was relatively happy with this arrangement.
>
> My ex-husband was living with another woman at the time we moved into the flats. I don't know how long it took for her to come around, but I think it was harder for her than it was for either of us. However awkward, once we all got over the hump, we found that we could make it work. It was clear to us that we had to see the world through our children's eyes. I think it worked because my ex-husband was very generous and I was very reasonable. He didn't want to have any more children, so I always had the sense that we were 'the Family' and that we were not going to be replaced.

I then asked Ingrid about the pros and cons of sharing a set of flats. She said that the pros of sharing the flats were:

> The children can and do see both parents on a daily basis and stay in the same neighborhood. The financial implication of the divorce can be mitigated. We also share the car under our divorce agreement, so we only have one car to maintain. The flats are near good schools. There is no big discrepancy between where the parents live. The children are not being shifted back and forth and don't have to go very far if they leave things in one flat or the other. The children's friends always know where to find them. We both have built-in childcare.

And that the cons were:

It was more difficult to make a new life and start over again. My sense is that if I had someone living with me it probably wouldn't have worked even if Keith was living with someone else. It's a fine line; that wasn't an issue for me but it would be a big complication if the two parties didn't get along as well as we did. It requires a great deal of give and take. It requires a great deal of maturity.

Although this arrangement worked for us, it certainly would not work for everyone. The cons were something that we had to give up, but overall it was worth it. I don't think we could have done this when we were young. I think one of the reasons that it worked was that we were not so scared that we couldn't make it work. Also we both have very good jobs and this has given us a tremendous amount of financial security. I once heard it said that, "The best gift a father can give his children is to treat their mother well." I can honestly say that my ex-husband Keith has treated me with respect and acknowledges my contribution to his life and to the lives of our children.

There was no or very little competition between us in deciding what was best for the children. I was the acknowledged person in charge of the children's day-to-day lives. Even though we divorced, we tried to give the girls a real sense of what a nuclear family was like. In fact, our 12-year-old thinks it's perfectly normal because this is the way we lived for the past eight years.

Taking it a year at a time provided us with the right balance of consistency to provide for a sense of stability, and enough flexibility that we could adapt to changes that occurred along the way.

Because the girls are older now and the three of us were beginning to feel cramped in the downstairs flat, we have now sold the flats. My ex-husband has a new girlfriend and she has her own house. So we debated the pros and cons of moving. On the negative side, if we moved into two separate residences, it would feel like getting divorced all over again, and none of us wanted that. On the other hand, we were cramped downstairs and my ex-husband was paying for a flat that he used less than half the time.

I knew of a house that was coming up for rent in our neighborhood, only two blocks away. It was a big house with an attic suite. Therefore, the move seemed to make sense as it would better suit all of our needs. We would have more room. It would cost my ex-husband less than the flat, but the amount would really be about equal because he would be paying more in child support and maintenance so we could afford the house. He would live in the attic suite about half the time, so it would provide him with enough time to spend with the girls who, as young teenagers, wanted to spend most of their time with their friends anyway. Once again, we decided to try this on a year-to-year basis, so no one would feel locked in if it didn't work.

I guess the only other issue was that our youngest daughter is really resistant to change. So I told her she would have veto power over the house. Luckily, when she saw the extra room that she would have, and learned that it was only two blocks away from the flats and her friends, she went for it.

Ingrid and Keith's story proves that with enough goodwill, flexibility, and maturity almost any type of arrangement is possible. Their willingness to brainstorm and experiment stood them in good stead. Trying novel arrangements for a one-year period allowed them to fairly evaluate all of the pros and cons and then make an informed decision whether to continue the arrangement or not.

Another couple, Ted and Alice, were married and then separated four years later. When I interviewed them 15 years later they were working on a formal separation agreement and may eventually get a formal divorce, but there is no urgency in this matter.

Ted and Alice have two children. At the time of the separation their daughter was two and their son was a newborn. Ted and Alice both describe their relationship as very amicable and from the start they were focused on what was best for their children, and on developing a mutual parenting arrangement that was as comfortable as possible for all of the parties involved.

The most unusual aspect of Ted and Alice's separation is that they purchased homes that were on two different streets, but the houses were back-to-back so that their homes shared the same back fence. Although they did not specifically look for houses that were back-to-back, when they realized that this arrangement was possible, they decided to try it, with the intention that if it worked, they would continue to live back-to-back until their children graduated from high school. Ted said that, "We had no occasion for going to court ever. We worked out property and agreed to maintenance [agreements] quite easily."

When I asked Ted if they put in a back gate so the children could move freely from house to house, he said that they actually tore down the fence because Alice and her mother — who eventually came to live with Alice — enjoy gardening and since both homes had rather small backyards, they decided to have one big backyard.

Alice had stayed off work for a year after each child was born and became the primary caregiver. Once there were two homes, the children tended to gravitate to Alice's house; they keep most of their books and clothes there, but the children were over at Ted's house several times a week. Last year their daughter moved in with Ted. She said that she wanted a quieter place to study. Ted says that he suspects that his daughter thought she would have more freedom at Ted's, although "more freedom at Ted's" may have turned out to be illusory.

Ted concluded by saying:

> At different times we have had other involvements and this put a little strain on the arrangement. However, we frankly discussed how we would handle other relationships and we did it specifically with a view to making life as comfortable for the children as possible. So overall it has worked very well and if it didn't work out, we had an out because we could have terminated [the agreement]. In fact, I think that some of the women I have dated had more trouble with it than either Alice or I did. Another thing that worked was that there was a lot of visiting back and forth, especially on holidays when there were family meals that included aunts, grandparents, and extended families members, so the children's extended family stayed intact.

> The most important thing is that both our children look at the arrangement positively. Our daughter has two places that she can be and she can be close to both parents, but at the same time, she is a teenager, who wants to be fiercely independent from her parents, except [for] the classic roles of dedicated chauffeur and bank machine. And I think my son would say that he is glad that both his parents are nearby and that they get along so well.

Maurine and Ian have three children. When they separated, the lived in the same house for two years. During that time, they lived as separately as possible under the same roof, and at the same time, they wanted to see if they could put their relationship back together. At the end of the two years, it became apparent that they could not make the relationship work, and they decided to formally separate. Maurine explained:

> By this time only our youngest daughter Clair was still at home and in grade 11. Since both of the older children had had the experience of living in the same home while attending high school, we decided to do the same for Clair, if at all possible. We decided to rent an apartment, so Clair could stay in the house and instead of the usual arrangement where the children moved from house to house, we decided to try a 15-day rotation, with each of us taking a turn living in the house with Clair, and then spending the rest of the time in the apartment. Although this arrangement was very disruptive for us, it did provide a great deal of stability for Clair. However, we felt very strongly that we wanted to give Clair the same degree of stability that we had given our other two children, and it was time-limited, because it would only last for two years at which time Clair would graduate from high school.
>
> For the next two years, we each spent half of our time in the apartment, and the rest of the time in the family home with Clair. Ian had the house from the first of the month to the morning of the 16th and I had the house from the afternoon of the 16th until the first of the following month.
>
> Since Ian earns approximately twice as much as I do, we pay in a ratio of two-thirds for Ian and one-third for me to cover all of the household expenses. For example, we are now getting the house ready to sell, and Ian is paying for two-thirds of the expenses of painting the house and I am paying one third. When we worked out our separation agreement, there was as much care and concern negotiating about the dogs as there was for everything else. In the end we got through it with an agreement we could live with and, most importantly, it was the best arrangement possible for Clair.
>
> I think it was doable because it was only for two years.

Maurine and Ian both commented that a certain amount of money and maturity is needed to make this arrangement work. According to both of them, the advantages are:

> Clair is so glad that it's this way. She says, "It's hard enough finding some of my things in one house, so I don't know how I could find them in two and my friends always know where to find me." We are also glad that all three children had the same upbringing and sense of having a stable home life, and that we are ending this arrangement at a logical time when Clair finishes high school.

Maurine also started that there are some disadvantages.

> Ian buys Clair unhealthy food and when I see it on our changeover days, it still gets me cross. Other disadvantages are that Ian and I have to have some form of personal interaction, having to do with the dogs and a shared house to deal with and negotiate about, in addition to our children. I would also say that it prolongs that finality phase.

When I asked Maurine how the dogs have adjusted, she laughed and said:

> So far they are just fine, however, when we sell the house this summer, each of us will keep one of the dogs and that will be an adjustment for them as they are so used to being together.

John says:

> Sometimes, a creative solution requires multiple generations to make it work.
>
> This is my second divorce. In my first marriage, I had a son, Patrick, and my ex-wife Sue has full custody. Sue has remarried and moved to another state so I see Patrick somewhat infrequently, really only once or twice a year and his stepfather, who is a very good man, is really his "psychological" father and I am kind of like a favorite uncle.
>
> In my second divorce, the situation is almost the exact opposite. My second ex-spouse moved to another state and I have full custody of our son Jody. To further my career, I wanted to go back to school and get an MBA. The problem was that I could afford neither the time nor the money. And then my Mom and Dad came to the rescue.

They invited Jody and me to live with them while I went back to school. Both Mom and Dad love Jody, and Mom, in particular, has been the only woman who was a constant in his life. Now I am about to take a position with a company that is located across the country. I know it will be difficult for Jody at first because he is so close to his grandparents, but I have promised him that we will come home to visit and that Gramps and Granny will come visit us. I will also get a video camera for my computer and my parent's computer so we can keep in close contact by phone, email, and webcam.

One way to summarize the characteristics of the thrivers I interviewed is that they all have three characteristics that I have seen over and over again of couples who are able to negotiate successfully. These characteristics are determination, flexibility, and maturity.

1. Determination

There was a story on the evening news that opened my eyes to the word "determination." The piece was about a homeless woman who was attending university. She had several part-time jobs, and the jobs paid for her tuition, books, and food. However, there was no money left for shelter, so she rode the buses at night because they were a safe place for her to sleep. She studied on the bus, and at the bus stops, before, between, and after classes. Her grades were A's and B's. If that isn't a story that exemplifies determination, I don't know what is.

Just like this heroic woman, the couples that negotiated successfully for themselves and their children had a remarkable amount of determination to make it work.

2. Flexibility

Flexibility is another hallmark of couples that negotiate successfully. Although they might not always have been able to be flexible in the short-term, they are flexible in the long-term. Flexible couples are more open to change and going with the flow. They are also more open to experimentation, because sometimes it is impossible to tell what will work and what will not until you try it. For example, different schedules may be needed as the children age and enter different stages of development. Couples also acknowledge they can go back to the old schedule if the new one does not work out.

3. Maturity

The quality of the relationship that the parents have with each other after they divorce will change as they mature and as their children mature. I remember constantly asking my son if he was alright after I moved out of the house. A few weeks later, he told me that it was like a bad cold which is worse at first. At that time, I would say he had more perspective on the situation than either of his parents.

I also had the most wonderful conversation with my daughter 12 years after the divorce. By this time she was in second-year university and I was able to visit her when I had some work near her school. Over dinner, we ended up talking about my and her mom's divorce. She told me that not only was she fine with it, she also said that there was not one thing she would change about it. The sense of relief I felt was palpable. One of the object lessons here is that maturity takes time and we have to wait because it can't be rushed.

4. Positive Precedents

In addition to determination, flexibility, and maturity, you and your ex-spouse will want to make sure that you negotiate positive precedents.

Although George and Beth's separation was very difficult at the time, when both of them looked back on it during my interview, they were surprised that they did so many things well — as Beth says, it all looks so easy in retrospect, but at the time when they were going through it, it all felt so terribly difficult.

When I asked George and Beth what worked, they said that they got off to a good start by seeing a mediator and then both parties got cooperative lawyers who had reputations of being able to work well together.

Beth said:

> At first, neither parent could bear not being with the children.

George said:

> I got an apartment nearby and at first we did two-day rotations. The two-day rotations worked well because the children were young and we lived only one block apart. Our nanny was able to go back and forth between the houses, which provided for a lot of consistency for all of

us. On the downside, the schedule was a bit disruptive, so when we got used to living in two households, we adopted a three-day-on and three-day-off arrangement, with Saturday night being negotiable. This arrangement worked well for a number of years, but as the children got older, it seemed like everything was always in the wrong house, so we switched to a week-on and week-off schedule, which at this time is working very well for all of us.

Often couples do not know ahead of time what will work for them and what will not because they are constantly, especially at first, moving into uncharted territory. Part of the flexibility that I have seen work for couples who have a successful parenting agreement is a willingness to experiment. It is through this willingness to experiment and to try different arrangements that a couple will be able to see concretely what will work and what will not, rather than going with a preconceived idea of what is right.

Both George and Beth appreciate the flexibility that they have been able to use in their scheduling arrangements. As long as both parties are willing to be reasonably flexible, then there is a lot of goodwill banked. If there have been numerous goodwill deposits, it is then much easier to ask for a withdrawal. If only one party is flexible, it is likely to lead to bad feelings and provide a poor role model for the children. On the other hand, a willingness to be flexible can lead to creative options as Irene's story points out.

I have full custody of my two children Adrian, who is 3, and Stephanie, who is 18 months. When Bobby and I separated, I just couldn't stand the thought of moving to an apartment where the children would not have their own backyard to play in. An apartment I could handle; not having a backyard, I could not.

My mother is a widow who still lives in her own house. I knew that although she puts on a very good face, she was very lonely without my Dad. I then thought if we could combine our two households and live together in one house or the other my babies could continue to have a backyard. The question was, would she be interested and, if so, which house would we keep?

I got up enough nerve and broached the subject with my mother. At first she was not very keen on the idea. As lonely as she was, she said that she valued her independence and did not want to put a strain on the very good relationship that we had. So I asked her to come and live with us for a month just to see what it would be like. I also suggested that at the end of the month she should move back to her house for a month before we made any type of major decision. I also said that if we did decide to live together, we could then choose one house or the other and try it for three to six months before deciding to sell either house.

When the month was over, and Mom went to move back to her place, we were both in tears. She had become so close to the kids that it was hard for her to leave. I maintained that she should live by herself for a month and then we could clearly decide if we should try it for a longer period of time, and that to be fair, maybe we should try living for a month in her house.

At the end of the next week, Mom came over and said that she had a surprise for me. She had talked to several real estate agents and had had her house assessed and was more than willing to sell. She said that with all the money she got from selling her house, we could have a little granny suite built onto my house and that way she could still have her independence. The only thing we would have to negotiate is who got to keep which piece of furniture.

I still thought that we should have a longer trial period, but Mom said that her mind was made up. I agreed, but there was one condition I wanted to have met.

Since my divorce, I had been seeing a counselor whom I really trusted and I wanted to make sure that we were doing the right thing. I asked Mom if she would go to several sessions with me so we could talk out all of the ramifications and plan for some of the inevitable setbacks that we would both face in taking such a bold step. At first she said that she didn't need to see a counselor, that her mind was made up, and the money could surely be spent on something more practical. I insisted, and in the end she came.

It has now been two years and things have worked out beautifully. Mom has her sense of independence; my children have a great backyard and neighborhood to grow up in. Yes, there is the occasional difference of opinion and sometimes there is tension between us, but the benefits far outweigh the costs.

Wally's story:

> Wally and Janice each had their three children half of the time. Wally decided to move his business from an office building into one of the upstairs bedrooms of his house in order to save time and money. With the money saved, Wally had two bedrooms, a separate entrance, and a shower built into the basement of his home. This gave his teenage sons more independence so they were all for it. His daughter wanted to stay upstairs with Dad; that way she only had to share the shower with one other person.

> Wally said that although he gets less work done when his children are with him, he more than makes up for the work when they are with their mother. He also says that he has now learned how to be a real father and a real parent to his children; the divorce forced him into it and he is very grateful that he realized how important it was for him to spend time with his children while he still has the opportunity.

Lynda and Mary-Beth's story:

> Both Lynda and Mary-Beth were living well below the poverty line. Both of their ex-husbands were frequently late with child support; both spent hours trying to stretch their meager budgets; and both were exhausted most of the time.

> Lynda and Mary-Beth knew each other by sight as both of their youngest children attended the same daycare. One day, both children were engaged in finishing their artwork, and the two mothers started chatting. Upon learning how much they had in common, they developed a friendship, and eventually became a built-in support group for each other. They started babysitting each other's children so they could have a break, since money for a babysitter was out of the question. This arrangement worked so well, that one day they broached the subject of living together. The savings in rent, food, heating, telephone, etc., would be enormous. However, the potential downside risk was also enormous. If it didn't work out, they would incur moving expenses that they could ill afford, and the likelihood of each finding new apartments that were as inexpensive as their current apartments was slim to nonexistent. Lastly, they had become great friends and confidants and they did not want to lose that either.

They decided to approach the possibility of their living together with great caution. Each family would bunk in with the other family for two weeks. They would then takea two week break. If they still thought that they might like to live together, they would try living together for four weeks. Although it was claustrophobic in their apartments, it worked well and the children loved it. Since they all agreed that the benefits of living together outweighed the sacrifices, they looked for and found an apartment that was big enough for both families.

At the time of the interview, they have been living together for five years. Mary-Beth has a steady boyfriend and they are thinking of living together at some time in the future. Both Mary-Beth and Lynda report that their ex-husbands have become somewhat more responsible, but the best news is that they no longer feel much anger or hostility towards their ex-husbands because each of them has become more independent.

5. Skills for Generating Creative Solutions

As can be seen from the preceding examples, innovation, flexibility, and creative thinking are important tools for all negotiators and problem solvers. Fortunately, these are learnable skills. There are six methods to help you learn to generate creative solutions, as covered in the following six sections.

5.1 Process examples of past creative solutions

The next time you get stuck trying to find the answer to a difficult problem, think of examples of previous solutions to other seemingly difficult problems and see if elements of those solutions can be applied to the present situation.

Exercise 1
Creative Solutions from the Past

List one or two creative solutions from the past that may help with a current or future negotiation with your ex-partner.

5.2 Consult with other creative thinkers

We all become used to looking at a problem in the same way, and sometimes we can't see our way out of the self-imposed boundaries we place on a particular problem.

For example, each of us has lost a set of glasses or keys. We turn the house upside down and cannot find the lost item anywhere. We ask another person to have a quick look for us, and within a short period of time, that person finds the missing item for us. The ability to look at a problem from a fresh perspective is often the key to solving an apparently unsolvable problem.

There are many creative solutions in the universe of possibilities. All one has to do is ask. Many people who have gone through this transition would be more then willing to help. As a courtesy, you can preface your question with a statement that if the other person is uncomfortable talking about it, that is perfectly all right.

You can also ask whether that person knows of anyone else who has faced and mastered a similar situation. For example, many of the people I interviewed for this book recommended that I talk to one of their divorced or separated friends and acquaintances. I always asked if they would first get permission for me to call. The result was that some of the best examples of creative solutions in this book were obtained by referrals. Likewise, you can consider your creative trusted friends and advisors as your Negotiation Yellow Pages. Then, when you get stuck for a creative solution, you just consult with your Yellow Pages.

Exercise 2
My Negotiation Yellow Pages

List the names of three to five people you could ask for assistance in finding creative solutions that would help you negotiate more effectively with your ex-partner.

1.

2.

3.

4.

5.

5.3 Read about creative solutions

There are books and magazines that contain wonderful examples of creative solutions. Read as many as you can and make a list of the solutions that strike you as creative. Selected books and resources are listed in the Resources section on the download kit included with this book.

5.4 Try to identify the mental model used to generate other creative solutions

One creative solution that was put forward at the Program for Negotiation for the American League Baseball strike of 1994–95 was to have a "virtual strike." In a virtual strike, the players would continue to play, but would receive only enough money to cover their expenses. Likewise, the owners of the ball teams would continue to receive enough money to cover their expenses. A neutral bank would hold all of the extra money. Every day that the players and owners did not settle, an increasingly large amount of the money that was put in escrow would be turned over to charity. For example, by the time $50 million had been accumulated, half of which would to be turned over to charity, there would be a tremendous amount of pressure on both sides to settle.

One way to learn how to find similar creative solutions in the future is by working backward to try to figure out how other problem solvers arrived at the solutions to their problems. As the original situation unfolded, both the players and the owners came to appear more and more greedy to the general public. The opposite of greed is charity. Therefore, the creators of this solution needed to look for a solution that had being charitable at its heart. In other words, how could the negative impression of being greedy be reframed positively? Reframing negatives into positives is one of the methods that can be used to help invent creative solutions.

5.5 Learn to use enhanced brainstorming

Brainstorming can be used to help us think outside of the box. The ground rules for brainstorming are that there is a set period of time, for example, 30 minutes, to say any idea that comes to mind and there should be absolutely no criticism. Often an idea that seems ill-conceived may be an innovative solution to a problem, can lead to an innovative idea, or it can be combined with other ideas to help resolve a problem.

Even though we know the rules of brainstorming, many times we silently criticize someone else's suggestion to ourselves and sometimes even criticize our own possible solutions without giving them a fair chance. One way to get around this natural tendency is to ask the other parties involved to come up with different ways to make someone else's suggestion or our own suggestion work, rather than to think about ways that it wouldn't work. Once again, no criticism is allowed in the brainstorming process.

Enhanced brainstorming uses brainstorming twice, once for the generation of ideas and a second time in how to implement those ideas. Enhanced brainstorming is more creative than regular brainstorming because we brainstorm both the ideas and how to implement those ideas. It also helps to make sure that we do not discard ideas that could work prematurely.

For example, both Ted and Julie wanted to have maximum contact with their two-and-a-half-year-old son Zach. One of the ideas they brainstormed was that one of them would work the night shift. They were about to discard this idea as out of hand, until they decided to use enhanced brainstorming. It was, in fact, possible for Ted to work on the night shift where he worked, but he would have to take a 20 percent cut in salary because there were no jobs in the night shift at his level of responsibility. However, if Ted and Julie pooled their income and took into account the cost of full-time daycare for Zach, then Ted's move to the night shift would not appreciably affect their income. In a few months, a position did open up in the night shift and Ted moved into that position. In the end, this proved to be an excellent solution, but they never would have considered it if they hadn't tried enhanced brainstorming.

5.6 Keep a creative solutions log

People who are good at telling jokes, such as stand-up comedians, keep a list of materials from which to draw. They also practice telling jokes, and learn how to use the right word and the right pause at the right time. Just as joke telling is a learned art, so is the art of creative problem solving. Keep a creative solutions log in which you write a description of the creative solutions and/or the mental models used to arrive at creative solutions, and then consult it the next time you are struggling to find a creative solution. You will be surprised at how often examples in your log can help you develop other creative solutions. For example, this book could be the start of your own creative solutions log.

Creative solutions allow you and your ex-spouse to better satisfy your and your children's same and differing needs, wants, goals and interests — but they do not happen by accident. Research has proven that the more stressed we are, the less likely we will be to develop creative solutions. The good news is that developing creative solutions is a skill that can be learned. We also know that it is a trial and error process, that there is a plethora of creative solutions in the universe, and that we can both learn from other people's creative solutions and we can ask for help in developing our own creative solutions. Creative solutions demand a creative negotiating process, which is covered in the next chapter.

2
Understand the Negotiation Process

Translating business negotiation strategies from the work setting to the family setting is clearly not appropriate in many situations. In fact, skilled negotiators, who can negotiate superb business deals, settle international conflicts, or negotiate the release of hostages, admit to completely blowing it at home when negotiating with a teenage son or daughter.

Even when we have been able to negotiate effectively, both at work and at home, the transition from being a spouse to being an ex-spouse is often a long and difficult one, especially in the beginning. During this transition the old rules of the marriage do not apply and the new rules of how to be divorced are yet to be formed and negotiated.

1. Six Reasons Negotiating May Be Poor

There are six reasons why the negotiation process is not used or is used poorly when it comes to negotiating with one's ex-spouse as discussed in the following sections.

1.1 Not fully understanding the negotiating process

The first mistake is not fully understanding the negotiating process. Although there are many books and courses on how to negotiate in business, not much has been written about the negotiating process for one's home or family life, especially from the point of view of ex-spouses who must negotiate on an ongoing basis. Therefore, people tend to translate their business negotiating strategies from the work setting to the family setting and sometimes that is clearly not appropriate.

Another option is to develop one's negotiating skills and strategies on a trial and error basis, and/or to rely on what we learned in our families of origin, and that may not be appropriate either.

1.2   Not applying what we do know to our negotiations

The second mistake is not applying what we do know to our negotiations with our ex-spouse. We know the process, but we forget to and/ or fail to apply what we do know. This occurs whenever we are so emotionally involved with the negotiation that we lose sight of the ultimate objectives of the negotiation. In other words, we may win the battle but lose the war.

1.3   Negotiating reactively rather than proactively because we allow ourselves to get emotionally hooked

The third mistake is negotiating reactively rather than proactively. One reason is that more is at stake when we negotiate within our families. I remember once, after having a particularly bad negotiation with my teenage son, I apologized for not listening well and letting it escalate way too quickly. I was then delighted when my son apologized to me for egging me on. After all, in intimate family relations we definitely know each other's hot buttons and areas of sensitivity. Therefore, it is sometimes all too easy to get emotionally hooked and negotiate reactively rather than proactively.

1.4   The negotiation process gets clouded by our anger over a real or perceived betrayal

The fourth mistake is allowing the negotiation process to get clouded by our anger over a real or perceived betrayal. There is often a profound sense of hurt and betrayal during the process of becoming separated and divorced. Often, both parties have put a lot of time, effort, and resources into building the relationship in the first place. There is often a tremendous sense of loss of the past, the present, and an imagined future. One of the findings from doing these interviews was that even when the current relationship with the ex-spouse was very good and one or both parties were in new and very satisfying relationships, there was invariably a point in the interview where the person I was interviewing got in touch with and expressed a deep sense of psychological pain as a result of talking about the break-up of that relationship, even though they now thought that the break up was necessary and resulted in their current happiness.

For others, the sense of pain was to some extent ongoing because it was related to feelings of being betrayed and deceived such as when one person found out that their spouse was having an affair when they, as a couple, were supposed to be working on improving their relationship; or a wife who gave up a promising career to be a stay-at-home mom, only to have her husband leave for a much younger woman after the children were grown. And, when there were children involved, in spite of the hurt and sense of betrayal, they still had to negotiate with their ex-spouse on a regular basis.

1.5 Not having an implementation system to help us consistently and thoroughly apply what we do know

The fifth mistake is not having an implementation system to help you consistently and thoroughly apply what you do know. Negotiating and influencing is a complex symphony of skills and all of those skills have to be used congruently and harmoniously to get the desired end result. It is also true that a chain is only as strong as its weakest link. If any part of the process is not as well developed as the rest, you will not negotiate as effectively as you could or should. And often, many people enter negotiations overly confident and underprepared.

1.6 Using positional bargaining in place of interest-based negotiating

The sixth mistake is to use positional bargaining. Positional bargaining is always stated in "either-or" language. Either the curfew is extended for an extra hour on the night of the junior high school prom or it is not. Either the ex-wife gets first choice for summer vacation dates with the children, or the ex-husband does. Interest-based negotiating is based on each party's underlying interests, and for almost all negotiations, there are multiple interests, and it is that multiplicity of interests that can give rise to developing creative solutions in order to maximize all of the parties' interests, and/or to judicious trade-offs that would still maximize the parties' interests when compared to positional bargaining.

In fact, one of the biggest mistakes that people make when entering into negotiations is that they have not done a good enough job in identifying their own and the other party's interests. Therefore, one of your first jobs in preparing for any negotiation is to identify your and the other party's interests.

2. Determining the Other Party's Interests Ahead of Negotiations

How do we determine interests? Interests underlay each partner's position for each issue that needs to be resolved. Interests are derived from our goals, expectations, aspirations, wants, needs, and fears. For example, let's say that your daughter, Stephanie, is doing very well in school and will enter high school next year. Dad wants Stephanie to attend private school like he did. Mom wants Stephanie to attend a public school like she did. One way to help resolve these types of issues is by looking at the underlying interests.

In positional bargaining there is one winner and one loser — either Dad gets his way and Stephanie goes to private school or Mom gets her way and Stephanie goes to public school. As the positions get entrenched, it becomes harder and harder to resolve the issue. To make matters worse, both parents can try to get Stephanie on their side, which can cause bad feelings not only between the parents, but also between one or both parents and Stephanie. Stephanie can side with Dad on this issue and then side with Mom on the next and/or learn to manipulate her parents to get more and more of what she wants and thereby eventually undermine the ability of both parents to parent.

An alternative approach to the private school/public school issue is to look at all of the parties' underlying interests and then see how those interests can be satisfied.

Mom's interests:

- Best academic experience.

- Best life experience.

- Doesn't want Stephanie to become a snob.

- Doesn't want to set a precedent that Stephanie's younger brothers and sisters will have to go to private school.

Dad's interests:

- Best academic experience.

- Best life experience.

- Wants Stephanie to develop excellent study and work skills.

- Wants Stephanie to develop academically as well as socially and recreationally through her extracurricular activities.

Stephanie's interests:

- Be with her friends.

- Do well in school but still have time for extracurricular activities.

Is there a way that the private school interests can be satisfied with the public school and vice versa? Perhaps Stephanie could go to private school, and belong to her local baseball team, which would allow her to keep and/or develop friendships with local children.

Likewise, is there a way that Stephanie could go to public school and still satisfy some of Dad's interests from private school? For example, Stephanie could go to summer school at the private school, or take honor classes in the public school, or learn a foreign language by going to summer school, etc.

3. Master Negotiator's Preparation Form

It is for these reasons, that the Master Negotiator's Preparation Form (MNPF) was developed. By using the MNPF you will begin your negotiations significantly better prepared with increased self-confidence resulting in greater self-control. After all, the reason that most New Year's resolutions fail is because there is no well-thought-out implementation plan. The MNPF will provide you with such a plan. The MNPF is based on the four components of interest-based negotiations as illustrated in Figure 1.

As the diagram indicates, negotiation is more of a circular process than a linear one. First there are the issues that brings you to the table. The issues could be relatively minor, such as, "Can I pick the kids up five minutes later today?," to relatively major, such as whether or

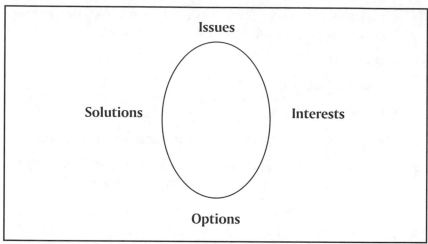

Figure 1: Four Components of Interest-Based Negotiations

not one parent should move to another state or province because of a career-enhancing job offer.

Next are interests, which tell you why you think and feel the issue is important to you and why you think it is important to your ex-spouse. The next step is brainstorming options to satisfy your and your ex-spouse's interests, and that brings you to an agreed-upon or sometimes an imposed solution. The reason I said that the process is circular rather than linear is that often we arrive at a solution only to find that one or both parties are resistant to putting that solution into practice. For example, there could be hidden interests on one or both sides; or there is more than one issue and those issues need to be negotiated concurrently; and/or the present negotiation triggers an incomplete negotiation from the past that has come to the surface, so the parties are negotiating multiple issues at the same time.

3.1 Case study using the Master Negotiators Preparation Form

The Master Negotiator's Preparation Form was created to ensure that both parties in the negotiation stop and think about what they really want and then come to the negotiation table as well prepared as possible. The form will also help both you and your ex-spouse develop more and better creative solutions to important problems that can affect you and your children for the rest of your lives.

Let us look at a complex case and discover how one divorcing couple, Ricardo and Sarah, used the MNPF to help resolve some very difficult issues. Ricardo went to work for Sarah's family business after they married. Ricardo proved to be a natural and worked his way up, helping the business double in size. Later, as Wally, Ricardo's boss and father-in-law, was nearing retirement, the family business developed a succession plan and Ricardo became the President and CEO.

As the business continued to prosper, Ricardo spent more and more time traveling and working on the business. Sarah and their two small children, Rory and Theo, began to feel more and more neglected. Things deteriorated until Ricardo and Sarah decided to divorce. At the time of the divorce, Ricardo was the majority shareholder owning 51 percent of the business, while the family owned 49 percent. Ricardo said:

Delicate only begins to describe the nature of the negotiations.

1. I was a well-known figure in a small town.

2. My father-in-law was a prominent figure.

3. There were small children involved: Rory, age 6, and Theo, age 8.

4. In the short-term at least, I needed to continue working with my ex-wife and father-in law in the family business.

5. I needed to negotiate a divorce, an employment contract with the business, and decide what to do with the business.

We were more financially interdependent than most divorcing couples because I worked for the family business. The family business couldn't immediately replace me, because no one else was trained in what I did nor had the contacts and relationships that I had developed that were necessary for the firm's continued performance. Also, this was a small town and there were no jobs available that would allow me to support myself and my family. To make matters even more complicated, at the point where Sarah and I were divorcing, I owned 51 percent of the business.

To help prepare Ricardo for these negotiations, I coached him in filling out the MNPF. Please note that the following is an overview of how to use the form. We will look at how the individual components work in more detail in the next chapters.

Sample 1
The Master Negotiator's Preparation Form™

My (Ricardo's) Interests	Their (Family's) Interests
1. Be the best father I can be	1. Make sure that the business continues to prosper.
2. Provide as much stability as I can for my family.	2. Wally wants to protect his daughter's interests. Sarah wants to protect her interests.
3. Maintain as much financial stability for my family and myself.	3. Protect the firm's reputation.
4. Develop both the best short-term and long- term settlement possible.	4. Protect their family's reputation in the community.
5. To let my ex-wife and her family know that I am truly sorry about what happened.	
My (Ricardo's) Prize (Ultimate Outcome)	**Their (Family's) Prize (Ultimate Outcome)**
In this case my short-term to medium-term goal is survival, to buy myself enough time to meet my responsibility to my ex-wife, and sort out what I need to do for myself, for my family, and for the business. To find a long-term arrangement that will work best for both the family and the business.	To ensure the long-term viability of the family business and to arrive at a divorce settlement that is in the best interests of Sarah and the children.
My (Ricardo's) Options	**Their (Family's) Options**
1. A one-year employment contract.	1. A one-year employment contract for Ricardo.
2. A two- or three-year, etc., employment contract.	2. A two- or three-year, etc., employment contract for Ricardo.
3. Buy the remaining shares from the family.	3. Buy the remaining shares from Ricardo.
4. A one-year employment contract renewable in one year increments.	4. Termination of Ricardo as President and CEO.
5. Any of the above with a 3-month or 6month early termination clause that could be triggered by either party.	5. Hire Ricardo as a consultant.
6. Set up annuities based on my equity in the business to pay for maintenance and child support.	6. Jointly work to sell the business.
7. Sell my shares of the business.	

Sample 1 — Continued

Standards/Objective Criteria

(Objective standards or objective criteria help the parties look at the negotiation much more objectively and make it easier to reach an agreement)

1. Determine as accurately as possible what it will cost to run two households.

2. Determine the amount of time and the dollar cost it would take to find someone who could do my job and train the person.

3. Arrive at an amount of support and maintenance based on state (provincial) guidelines.

ZOPA (Zone of Possible Agreement)

- *Aspire to?*

  (The best arrangement you could get)

  Continue to work in the business until an ideal time to transition out of the business.

- *Content with? (Satisfactory)*

  Continue to work in the business for the next year or so.

- *Live with? (Acceptable minimal settlement)*

  Sell my shares in the business immediately.

My (Ricardo's) BATNA (Best Alternative To a Negotiated Agreement)	Their (Family's) BATNA (Best Alternative To a Negotiated Agreement)
In this case my BATNA is also my WATNA. Going to court and having a long drawn out adversarial proceeding is not in anyone's best interests. My applying for work outside of the family firm is also not in anyone's best interest in the short term.	Terminate Ricardo's contract. Sell the business to a third party. Terminating Ricardo's employment and/or selling the business was not in the family's best interests either personally, financially, nor from the point of view of Wally, who very much wanted to retire.
My (Ricardo's) Leverage	**Their (Family's) Leverage**
Although I do not want to use it, the cost to my family and the cost to the business if I were to leave the company now and/ or sell my shares to a third party which would lessen the family's control over the business.	In the short term, the family has financial leverage until Ricardo finds a new position. The family could also try to force Ricardo out of his position as President/CEO before he is ready to go.

Sample 1 — Continued

My (Ricardo's) Trade-Offs/Concessions	Their (Family's) Trade-Offs/ Concessions
One trade-off is my and our sense of privacy as our divorce will be very public in our small town. I am prepared to take a major cut in my standard of living to support my children. I am prepared to sacrifice a certain amount of personal happiness in order to make this work over the next three or four years.	The family is prepared to lose a certain amount of their sense of privacy to make this work.
Type of Relationship I would like to have with my Partner during the Negotiation and long-term	**Type of Relationship I would like to have with my Partner during the Negotiation and long-term**
Cooperative	Cooperative
My Partner's Negotiation Style is	
My ex-father in law is a very principled man and for the most part he would like to work with me cooperatively to salvage the business. On the other hand, he feels hurtand betrayed, and as a father he also wants to protect his daughter. My ex-wife Sarahfeels incredibly hurt and betrayed. Her style reflects her mixed feelings. One minuteshe is on board with making this work for the sake of the family business, the next, she-wants me completely out of her life and out of her community.	
The style I will use in this negotiation is:	
I will endeavor to negotiate as cooperatively as I possibly can as it is in everyone's best interests that I do so.	
My Opening Statement	
I am truly sorry for any of the pain that I have caused you and your family. At the sametime we both have an obligation to our two children to provide them with as much love,stability and continuity as possible. I am prepared to discuss any and all options thatwould accomplish this and hope that we can work out a settlement that will be in our best interests as a family and as a business.	

A blank copy of the MNPF can be found in the download kit included with this book, or you can purchase the Master Negotiator's Digital Coach and Workbook, from www.bradmcrae.com.

Both Ricardo and Sarah said that using the Master Negotiator's Preparation Form helped them be more objective; negotiate more civilly; preserve their relationships with their children; save time and money; and reach closure sooner than they would have been able to do without using the form.

4. Choice Points

A choice point is an incredibly important point in the negotiation whereby if the party or parties do the right thing, in the right way, at the right time, the negotiation will move toward an effective resolution. On the other hand, if the party or parties do the wrong thing, in the wrong way, at the wrong time, the negotiation will be jeopardized because the dispute will escalate, the party or parties become more positional, and/or the negotiation will break off entirely.

Choice points and the leverage that choice points have to move a negotiation in a positive or negative direction is one of a negotiator's most important skills. For example, apologizing for a word said in the heat of an argument, acknowledging the other party's pain, and/or acknowledging the progress that has been made in other areas can all have a positive effect on the negotiation process — as can getting angry and applying more power and more force than necessary — choice points are points of maximum leverage. Learn to be aware of them and use them wisely.

Choice points can sometimes be identified before entering into a negotiation, but at other times will only become apparent during a negotiation, and sometimes, only after the negotiation. Even if it is after the negotiation, you are still making progress, because it increases the likelihood that you will be able to identify the choice points before or during the negotiation the next time.

There were two critical choice points in this negotiation that led to a cooperative solution that helped maximize the parties' interests. The first critical point was Ricardo's offer to sell two percent of the business back to the family. The net result was that Ricardo was able to maintain the financial stability he wanted for his family and for himself. Both he and the family were able to work out a three-year transition plan at which time he left the family business. Using the MNPF helped all of the parties look at their situation more objectively and proactively.

The second crucial choice point was the family changing lawyers. Ricardo reported:

> My ex-wife and her father used the same lawyer for the divorce and the business. He was very confrontational and aggressive. He was the kind of guy who, when he played sports, had to win. He was very combative and turned it into a turf war. For him, it was a game, winning was the only option, and it didn't matter who the casualties were, including our children. He really had it in for me and for my lawyers as well. I should add that I used two separate lawyers; one for the divorce and one for our business dealings.
>
> Eventually he went so far that my ex-wife and her parents decided that it couldn't continue. They fired the aggressive lawyer and hired a much more cooperative lawyer. Although the negotiations had their difficult issues to negotiate, we achieved a settlement that we all felt was fairly reasonable and her changing lawyers did a lot to repair the damage to our relationship that her first lawyer caused.

One of the most important things that we can learn from Ricardo and Sarah's experience is that ex-spouses who have had children together will have to get along for many years after the divorce. In fact, the divorce settlement and the separation agreement are the foundation for what the future relationship will be built upon. You will have to live on top of that foundation for a much longer period of time than the lawyers will, so choose your lawyers carefully.

There is another concept that is vital to the negotiation process and that is the concept of meta-negotiation.

5. Meta-Negotiation

The prefix "meta" means "about itself." Therefore, a meta-negotiation is a negotiation about how we are going to negotiate. For example, a husband and wife who are divorcing could each hire aggressive lawyers to represent them, however, that could result in an escalation of their conflict whereby they could end up with a very expensive suboptimal solution. On the other hand, they could see a mediator with the intention of maximizing their resources, minimizing their expenses, and developing the best parenting relationship possible for the sake of their children. In summary, a couple who is divorcing will find that from time to time they engage in both cooperative and adversarial bargaining. However, underlying both types of bargaining, they will negotiate which style of negotiation will pervade their negotiations. Choosing the style is a meta-negotiation.

Beware of mixed messages. If you say that you want to have a cooperative negotiation with your ex-spouse and at the same time you are being indiscriminate about sharing information that your ex-spouse thought was private, your ex-spouse will, like most people, believe the latter rather than the former. This type of mixed message can and will affect the tone and progress of all subsequent negotiations.

Exercise 3
Choice Points

Think back and give two or three examples where you used choice points wisely in your negotiations with your ex-partner.

1. _____

2. _____

3. _____

Think back and give two or three examples where you didn't use choice points wisely in your negotiations with your ex-partner.

1. _____

2. _____

3. _____

Now let's be proactive. Identify three possible choice points in your up and coming negotiations.

1. _____

2. _____

3. _____

3

Develop a Negotiating Plan

One of the main values of preparation is determining if negotiation is necessary or if there are other courses of action that can be taken to resolve the issue. If negotiation is necessary, then being fully prepared will make you more like master negotiators, who come to the table incredibly well prepared while their more amateur counterparts come to the table overly confident and underprepared. It is much better to find out that you need to do more preparation before rather than during the negotiation.

I developed the Master Negotiator's Preparation Form (MNPF) to assist you in coming to the table as well prepared as possible. That said, no one would want to use the MNPF for every negotiation he or she is in, as that would clearly be a great waste of time. For most negotiations, you may only need to fill in certain sections in order to be as well prepared as necessary for that negotiation, however, for the more important negotiations you will want to fill it in completely.

In addition, for your most important negotiations, not only will you want to complete the MNPF, you will want to go over the form with a trusted advisor or advisors to make sure that you fully understand each element of the form for the negotiation. It is very likely that your advisor may be able to identify interests, options, trade-offs, and concessions that you may never have thought of in a million years. This is why master negotiators know the importance of having a pool of people who can help them prepare for their negotiations (your Negotiation Yellow Pages, as discussed in Chapter 2).

You may want to consider doing a mock role-play of the negotiation with a trusted friend or advisor. No one would star in a play and only show up on opening night.

There would be rehearsal after rehearsal. Role-playing your particular negotiation both as yourself and as your ex-spouse will give you a unique perspective as to how well prepared you are. It will also help flesh out some of the questions that you need to ask and that will be asked of you. Issues that have to be further explored and researched will quickly become evident. In sum, the true value of the MNPF is that you can now prepare in a systematic manner rather than in an ad hoc one.

There are five crucial elements in the negotiation process. The first is the type of relationship you would like to have with your ex-spouse or ex-partner during the short-term and during the long-term. The second is to identify your partner's negotiation style. The third is to identify the negotiation style you will use in the negotiation. The fourth is muscle level or how much power or force you will use in the negotiation, and the fifth is to develop your opening statement.

What type of relationship would you like to have with your ex-spouse during the short-term and long-term? The answer to this question will help you look at the negotiating process more proactively. In fact, the more I study the negotiation process and master negotiators, the more long-term my outlook has become. One of the things that the divorcing and separating couples I interviewed said again and again was to be very careful about burning bridges because you never know when you will need to cross over that bridge again. The other expression that is apropos here is that we can all learn to disagree without being disagreeable. For example, Jeff lost his temper with his ex-wife Alana when he found out she forgot to bring over their son's hockey equipment. This meant that Jeff and their son would be late for the playoff game. Two nights later, Jeff found out that he had been scheduled to make an out-of-town business trip for the following week. Only the following week it was his turn to look after their two children. He sheepishly had to ask Alana to change their schedule regarding who looks after the children. Eventually she said yes, but the cost to Jeff was a sizable concession in the amount of time he got to spend with their children.

You can enhance your relationship with your ex-spouse by being courteous, respectful, listening attentively, and being open to persuasion.

In fact one of the best ways to get the other party to be open is to be open to persuasion yourself.

Your reputation as a negotiator is one of the most important assets you have. Every time you enhance your reputation, it's like putting money in the bank. Likewise, every time you diminish your reputation, it's like taking money out.

1. Ten Concepts

In order to negotiate as effectively as possible, there are 10 concepts in the negotiation process with which you will want to become very familiar as discussed in the following ten sections.

1.1 Issues versus positions

An issue is a concern or a problem that a divorcing or separating couple has to deal with, and there are literally hundreds, if not thousands, of issues or potential issues. Examples of issues are:

- Should your son or daughter have any discretionary items such as an MP3 Player, cell phone or Xbox? If yes, who pays and how much?

- How much time should your son or daughter spend watching television?

- How much time should your son or daughter spend on the computer?

- Should your son or daughter get his or her driver's license?

- What types of clothing should your son or daughter wears?

- How much money should be spent on your son's or daughter's clothing?

- What time does your son or daughter have to be in after the school dance?

- Should your son or daughter be allowed or encouraged to work part-time?

With positions there are often strong feelings as to what is right, wrong, proper, improper, doable, not doable, good, bad, appropriate, inappropriate, suitable, unsuitable, etc., attached to that issue. In other words, while issues are neutral, they become positions when there is some emotional feeling or a sense of entitlement attached to them. Examples of potential positions are:

- Since you are never on time, I am going to cancel your visitation rights.

- There is no question; our daughter will get confirmed in my church.

- I don't care if our son is not a star student; he does not have to give up any of his sports.

- I don't care if this is your summer to have first choice of when you take your summer vacation, our family is having a family reunion the last week of August and the children will be attending.

For example, a recent newspaper article recounted the sad tale of a five-year-old boy named Jeff. His parents, Francoise and Nick, separated when Jeff was three years old. There had been a great deal of conflict when they were married and it got worse when they separated. However, they managed to keep most of their differences to themselves until it was time for Nick to go to school. Francoise was French speaking and she desperately wanted Jeff to go to school in total immersion where he could continue to learn French. Nick was equally adamant that Jeff had to have all of his schooling in English. Both Francoise and Nick went to the library and the Internet to bolster their respective cases. Jan argued that learning a second language would help their son learn to respect diversity and would broaden his horizons. Nick argued that being in French Immersion would result in poorer skills in English, math, and science.

Since neither party would concede to the other party's "superior" arguments, they asked their respective lawyers to become involved. In the meantime, school was starting and Francoise enrolled Jeff in French Immersion. Nick went to court asking for an injunction that would require Francoise to put Jeff in an all-English program. The result of all of this conflict and tension took its toll on Jeff. He became more and more withdrawn, both at home and at school. In fact he became so preoccupied that the teacher asked for a conference with both parents.

A much better way to resolve disputes and conflicts is with interest-based negotiation, and that is the topic to which we turn next.

1.2 Identifying your and your ex-partner's interests

Identifying your and your ex-partner's interests is key to developing creative options and negotiating successfully. One of the best analogies I have heard is that negotiations are like puzzles; the interests are the pieces, and the negotiator's job is to figure out how to put the pieces (interests) together creatively. However, unlike a puzzle, there is more than one way to put the pieces together in a negotiation.

The difference between positions and interests is one of the most crucial and difficult tasks for a negotiator to learn. Generally speaking, a position is stated in "either/or" language; for example, the solutions will be either your solution or mine. Positional bargaining tends to be rigid and adversarial. Interest-based bargaining tends to be much more creative and flexible because there usually are many interests underlying positions. Research has demonstrated that interest-based bargaining is 90 percent more likely to result in creative and optimal solutions. In Francoise and Nick's case, both parents have similar interests. They wanted Jeff to get the best education possible, to enjoy school, and get off to a good start. They also both wanted Jeff to develop a healthy self-esteem. Once their interests were identified they found that they had more in common than they thought. In fact, master negotiators are four times more likely to identify common ground and we are much more likely to identify common ground at the level of interests than at the level of positions.

Although identifying interests is integral to the negotiating process, one of the most common mistakes that negotiators make is not accurately or thoroughly identifying both parties' interests. Interests answer the question as to why a particular issue is important to us. More specifically, interests are based on one's goals, expectations, aspirations, wants, needs, desires, and fears. To counteract the tendency of not identifying enough of both party's interests, I suggest you use the Rule of Four.

The Rule of Four is a rule of thumb that suggests that most people do not negotiate as well as they could or should because they fail to identify enough of their own or the other party's interests. Therefore the rule suggests that we identify at least four of our own and four of the other party's interests. In truth, there may be fewer interests or there may be many more. By using the rule of four and setting a minimum target, you are more likely to list your most important interests. Likewise, most negotiators only identify one or two options to satisfy all of the parties' interests and this can often lead to suboptimal solutions. So the rule of four can and should be applied to generating options, developing your Best Alternative To A Negotiated Agreement (BATNA), and coming up with a minimal number of standards and objective criteria, all of which will help you negotiate more effectively than if you did not use the role of four as a guide.

Let's go back to the case of Nick and Francoise's conflict as to whether their son, Jeff, should start school in English or French. Instead of being positional and reactive, Nick and Francoise decided to see a mediator. The mediator helped them articulate the interests underlying their position (see Table 1).

Table 1
Identifying Interests

Mom's (Francoise's) Interests	Dad's (Nick's) Interests
Jeff will like and adapt well to school.	Jeff will like and adapt well to school.
Jeff will learn to appreciate my French heritage.	Jeff will be able to develop friends and feel like he fits in.
Jeff will get a broad education.	Jeff will get a solid foundation that will help him as he advances in school.
Jeff will be able to easily go to day care after school.	Jeff will be able to easily go to daycare after school.

Often it is also helpful to prioritize the parties' interests. In this case, the interests were prioritized, and if they weren't already, the parties could number their interests as which was the number one, number two, etc., or if some of the interests were very similar in rankings, they could be ordered in descending levels of importance such as "A" interests, "B" interests, "C" interests, etc.

1.3 What is the prize?

The prize is the ultimate outcome you want from the negotiation. It is not the same as your interests. The prize can be at a concrete level, an abstract level, or both. For example, in the case of Jeff's schooling, the prize at a concrete level is to put him in a school where he would be happy and get a good education. The prize at an abstract level is to enhance his self-confidence and self-esteem. By having a creative, mutually acceptable outcome, he will feel freer to approach his parents with problems that will arise in the future. Also, in this negotiation, they have an optimal outcome that can serve as a mental model for creative solutions that they can use and/or modify to help in future negotiations.

1.4 What are the options?

Options refer to options for a settlement at the negotiating table. Options are developed by brainstorming. The three rules for brainstorming are: (a) no criticism, (b) every option is worth considering, and (c) deciding which options are valid takes place only after the brainstorming session is completed.

Two rules that Master Negotiators use are the Rule of Four and Going Wide before Going Deep. As stated above, you are not ready to negotiate unless you have identified four options (as well as four interests). In truth, the number four is arbitrary, you may only come up with one or two options, or you may need to develop 20. The purpose of the rule is that most of the thousands of people I have observed negotiating come to the table with too few options and the final solution is less robust and less creative than it could or should have been, because there were gains that one or both parties left on the table. In other words, the pie was not expanded to the degree that it could have been. By identifying at least four options, the parties are more likely to be able to identify options or to combine options to arrive at optimal solutions that do not leave gains on the table.

Go Wide before Going Deep stipulates that we want to get all of the options on the table before we start exploring any of them in detail. Once we start evaluating those ideas in detail we become more critical and less creative. Therefore, to truly enhance the brainstorming process and to get as many creative ideas on the table as possible, we need to continue the brainstorming process (going wide) before we start evaluating and/or criticizing each idea's worth (going deep).

There will also be times when neither party will be able to think of creative solutions. In cases like this, the parties should take a break from the table and/or ask for creative ideas from third parties. Taking a break from the table is often helpful. All of us can relate to the time we took a break and then when we were not consciously trying to solve the problem, had an "aha" or "eureka" insight that helped solve the problem. Likewise, we have all had the experience when we thought a negotiation was hopeless; however, when we mentioned the issue that was deadlocking the negotiation to a friend or advisor, that person came up with a creative solution that resolved the problem.

Let us look at an example where the use of the Rule of Four to develop options and going wide before going deep can help enrich the debate by developing creative options to maximize all of the parties' interests. For example, take Stephanie from the example in Chapter 2, who is doing very well in school and will enter high school next year. Dad wants Stephanie to attend private school like he did. Mom wants Stephanie to attend a public school like she did. One way to help resolve these types of issues is to look at everyone's underlying interests. In positional bargaining there is one winner and one loser — either Dad gets his way and Stephanie goes to private school or Mom gets her way and Stephanie goes to public school. As the positions get entrenched it becomes harder and harder to resolve the issue. To make matters worse, both parents can try to get Stephanie on their side, which can cause bad feelings not only between the parents, but also between one or both parents and Stephanie. Stephanie can side with Dad on this issue, and then side with Mom on the next and/or learn to manipulate her parents to get more and more of what she wants and thereby eventually undermine the ability of both parents to parent.

An alternative approach to the public/private school issue is to look at all of the parties' underlying interests and then see how those interests can be satisfied.

Is there a way that the private school interests can be satisfied with the public school and vice versa?

To recap, it is possible: Stephanie could go to private school, and belong to her local baseball team, which would allow her to keep and/or develop friendships with neighborhood children. Another option would be to do some volunteer work if the issue was being too economically isolated. Likewise, is there a way that Stephanie could go to public school and still satisfy some of Dad's interests from private school? For example, Stephanie could take the International Baccalaureate program in the public school system, or take honor classes in the public school, or learn French by going to summer school in France or go to summer school at the private school and see if she likes it or not. In this and many other cases, if the ex-spouses can come up with enough options, they can find a solution or solutions that are robust enough that there are not winners and losers because everyone's interests can be well, or at least reasonably well-satisfied.

1.5 What are the standards and objective criteria?

Many difficult negotiations can be made much easier through the judicious use of objective criteria. Three advantages of using objective criteria are:

1. It helps the participants step back and take a more objective look at their concerns.

2. It adds a new perspective or way of looking at a problem.

3. It helps the parties save face as they move from their original positions to a new solution.

Let's suppose a divorcing couple has one car, a 2004 Honda Civic, and they have to determine its true market value as part of the settlement. Rather than pick a price out of thin air, they both could look up the retail value of the car and that would be one possible standard. They could also go to the classified section of their local newspaper and see what comparable cars were selling for, and/or they could go online and get an estimate of what the car was worth. And there are many other standards they could look at, such as the recommended selling price in books like *Lemon Aid*.

These objective standards could help them determine a range in which the selling/purchase price of the car should reside. However, most sources have different prices depending on which options the car has and how good or poor shape the car is in. Therefore, many times the focus of the negotiation is how one can agree as to which standard or standards should be applied in each particular negotiation. For example, the husband asserts that the car is in superb shape and the wife asserts that the car is in poor shape. In most cases their mutually different assertion would derail the negotiations. However, they could take the car and have it assessed by an independent mechanic. Using the mechanic's assessment as to the condition of the car would be a creative use of objective criteria.

1.6 Are there robust and elegant solutions?

A robust solution is a solution that maximizes each party's interests. The pie has been expanded and there are no gains left on the table. To qualify as an elegant solution, it must have a good substantive outcome, a good relationship outcome, and have used the best process for the negotiation. Elegant solutions are so good that they become models for future negotiations. A good example of an outcome that is neither robust nor elegant is two parents who continue to fight each other in court; everyone in the family becomes damaged by the process, and it uses up all of the family's monetary resources. An example of a solution that is both robust and elegant follows.

> I do volunteer work in Jamaica several times a year. It was my daughter Katie's last year of high school and I was going to be in Jamaica during Katie's March break, so I invited her to come to Jamaica with me. We would have some time to travel around the island and Katie could stay in the hotel and relax for the two days that I was teaching at the University College of the Caribbean.

> However, there was one major problem. Katie was working to complete her Grade 10 piano which meant that she needed to practice the piano for two hours per day. Katie felt torn between piano and Jamaica. I called every major hotel in Kingston, until I found the Pegasus Hotel. This was the one hotel that had a piano and they said that Katie could practice every morning between 6:00 and 8:00. Everyone's interests were very well satisfied. When I inquired about the extra charge, the hotel manager, who was also a former piano student, said it was on the house.

1.7 Best Alternative To a Negotiated Agreement (BATNA)

Your Best Alternative To a Negotiated Agreement (BATNA) is your walk-away alternative. Your BATNA is what you will do if you can't reach an agreement. One good way to put your BATNA into perspective is to imagine the worst case scenario.

For example, after Lenny and Rose separated, Lenny noticed that sometimes when he called Rose in the evenings, she would start to slur her words. As time went on, the slurring of words became more and more frequent and the onset of the slurring of the words happened earlier and earlier. Finally, one day, Lenny noticed that the front end of Rose's car had been smashed in. Rose reported that she had been in a minor car accident and that "no," it was not her fault.

Lenny tried, on numerous occasions, to discuss Rose's alleged drinking, but she never wanted to talk about it and got increasingly defensive and angry when Lenny brought it up. Lenny was becoming frantic. His worst fear was that if Rose drove while intoxicated, their three children could be hurt. Since there was no negotiating about this issue, Lenny had to develop a BATNA. Lenny and his lawyer drafted a carefully written document and sent it to Rose's lawyer stating that Lenny would apply for full custody unless there could be an independent assessment of Rose's drinking.

However, just because you have a BATNA, does not mean that you should use it. If fact, if both parties' BATNAs are clearly unattractive, you may have a Worst Alternative To A Negotiated Agreement (WATNA).

1.8 Worst Alternative To A Negotiated Agreement (WATNA)

A Worst Alternative To a Negotiated Agreement (WATNA) is a powerful technique to get the parties back to the table and bargaining in good faith because the WATNA is a clearly unattractive outcome for all of the parties involved. WATNA helps the disputing parties see how attractive it is to have a negotiated, mediated, or arbitrated outcome. For example, a divorcing couple may continually fight about a financial settlement; however, if they tie it up in litigation for the next four to five years, neither of them is likely to have anything left. Or, two former spouses who are busy fighting over the remains of their relationship may mean that neither one has the time or energy to start a relationship where one or both parties could become very happy.

1.9 Zone of Possible Agreement (ZOPA)

Master negotiators know that there is a Zone Of Possible Agreement (ZOPA), and that by remaining flexible they will increase their chances of reaching an agreement, and that the particular agreement is more likely to be robust. Therefore having a ZOPA is much better than having one positional outcome and miss out on the possibility of creating an innovative solution that could better meet the needs of both parties.

ZOPAs help negotiators think outside the box. It describes the multiplicity of options and outcomes that lie within the grasp of skillful negotiators. Some of these options and outcomes favor you more, others your ex-spouse, and still others both parties fairly equally. When you look at your ZOPA, there are at least three points to consider. The first point is, "To what do you aspire?" What you aspire to is close to the best arrangement you could get. The second point is, "With what would you be content?" The third point is, "With what you could live?" But getting to an offer that you could live with means that you are getting close to a best alternative, or BATNA territory. In other words, you are getting near to the point where your BATNA or walk-away alternative is more attractive than the deal currently on the table.

Master negotiators also are vigilant in seeing if there is a way to boost their BATNA so that their BATNA is better than the minimally acceptable deal that has been tabled.

For example, Sarah and her new husband John moved into a two-bedroom condominium in the suburbs right after her youngest daughter, Ariel, left for university. Sarah's ex-husband Billy remained in his house which was in the neighborhood where both of their children grew up and where almost all of their friends lived. When Ariel came home for the Christmas holidays, it was not clear where Ariel would stay. When both her parents lived in the same neighborhood, she would spend an equal amount of time at both parents' homes. However, Ariel wanted to spend most of her time in her old neighborhood so she could maximize the time she spent with her friends.

In looking at her ZOPA, the best deal that Sarah thought she could get was to have Ariel stay with her half the time and stay with her ex-husband half the time. The minimally acceptable deal for Sarah was that Ariel would stay at her father's most if not all of the time, and Sarah could take Ariel out shopping and/or out for meals. However, when people put their heads together, they came up with an alternative that best satisfied everyone's interests. Since Ariel wanted to spend most of the time at her Dad's house (which would give her more time with her friends), they all agreed that Sarah could pick Ariel up from the airport and drop her off at the airport. This gave Ariel and her mom some of that very important one-on-one time. Ariel would also spend three nights at her mom's, which included the night before Christmas. Staying at her dad's house also gave dad that important one-on-one time with Ariel. By fully exploring their ZOPA, all of the parties were able to come up with a more creative solution. A graphical representation of Sarah's ZOPA appears in Figure 2.

1.10 Trade-offs and concessions

Negotiations are often about trade-offs and concessions. By writing down your trade-offs/concessions you will be more likely to make sure that you have at least four options; it forces you to think of the priority

Aspire to ...

spend half-time with Ariel

Content with ...

three nights with Ariel, plus pick-up from airport, additional times together for lunch, dinner and other activities such as shopping

Live with ...

pick-up from airport, plus several lunches and dinners both at my house and in restaurants, and one additional outing such as shopping

Figure 2: Zone of Possible Agreements (ZOPA) for Sarah

in which you should offer your trade-offs/concessions, and it protects you from putting offers on the table prematurely and/or from being overly generous.

For example, if I am negotiating with my ex-spouse, and we suddenly have a breakthrough in the negotiations because my ex-spouse puts a creative solution on the table, then if I reward my ex-spouse by putting a concession on the table, and subsequently realize that I am being too generous, it is very difficult to take that concession off the table.

Last, when you prepare with a trusted friend or advisor, he or she may see a concession that you could make that would be of great benefit to your ex-spouse and of little cost to you, or a concession that your ex-spouse could make that could be of great benefit to you at little cost to your ex-spouse. My workshop participants find that one of the most important lessons they have learned came from being coached on finding more creative trade-offs and/or concessions.

By keeping track of your trade-offs and concessions and the trade-offs and concessions of your ex-spouse, you are more likely to make sure that they are reasonably equal and you will be less likely to be taken advantage of. It is also true that at some point in the negotiation process, it may be prudent to concede a little more on one negotiation in order to get a little more on another. However, this is more likely to be true if you are dealing with a cooperative rather that an aggressive negotiator because the cooperative negotiator is more likely to reciprocate and the aggressive negotiator is more likely not to reciprocate.

We will go into more detail as to how negotiation style affects the negotiation process in Chapter 5.

2. Five Variables in Negotiation Relationships

These 10 concepts we just covered about the negotiation process take us from issues to interests to options to solutions and back again. However, we must ask ourselves what type of negotiation relationship we wish to have with our ex-spouses. There are five relationship variables that must be taken into account to ensure that we negotiate as well as we possibly can as covered in the following five sections.

2.1 What is my negotiation style?

Identifying our own negotiation styles is a hard thing to do. This is complicated by the fact that we may use different or slightly different styles in differing situations. We also may use a different style or a somewhat different style in public versus private settings.

A colleague of mine, Linda Edgecomb, often asks her audiences if they are better parents in public settings than they are in private settings. Style trumps substance almost every time, so it is essential that we control our negotiation styles and make them work for us rather than against us. Style is so important that Chapter 5 is devoted entirely to this subject.

2.2 What is my ex-spouse's style?

Master negotiators assess their ex-partner's negotiation styles as early as possible in the negotiation. Diagnosing your partner's negotiating style is critical because you will then be able to choose your style, and the elements therein, in a more strategic and proactive manner than in a reactive manner. Note that your ex-partner's style may vary from negotiation to negotiation or even within the same negotiation. Make sure to reassess his or her style both at the outset and during each negotiating session.

2.3 Which negotiation style should I use?

Your negotiation style is critical because it will pervade every aspect of your negotiation and it is important to choose the style that you will use in a particular negotiation proactively rather than reactively. By carefully choosing your negotiation style you will negotiate far more effectively in both the short term and in the long term. Integrally related to your negotiation style is your muscle level.

2.4 Muscle level

Muscle level is how much force or power you need to bring to the negotiating table. There are two mistakes made with muscle level: too much too soon and too little too late. Therefore, one of the best things you can do is write down how much force or power you are going to use and the order in which you are going to use it. This is especially true if you find that you are getting angry. By writing down what you will do at each muscle level, you are more likely to escalate consciously rather than unconsciously.

For example, Randy, a non-custodial parent, was having a great deal of difficulty getting his ex-wife Lenore to stick to their legal visitation schedule. Randy was supposed to get his two children every Wednesday night and every other weekend from Friday evening until Monday morning when the girls went to school. However, Lenore would often call Randy at work Wednesday afternoon and tell him that the girls were panicked because they had too much homework to do or a test to study for. Lenore had also developed the habit of booking the girls' doctor appointments and dental appointments for late Friday afternoons and this was taking away from Randy's time with his daughters as well. By keeping baseline data, Randy was able to show that while each incident did not take up much time, the cumulative effect was substantial. When Randy listed his muscle levels, it looked like this:

1. Verbal request to stick to the agreement.

2. Verbal request to stick to their agreement with baseline data documenting the time he was losing with his daughters on a yearly basis.

3. Written request to stick to their agreement with baseline data documenting the time he was losing with his daughters on a yearly basis.

4. Written request from Randy's lawyer to Lenore's lawyer requesting that Lenore honor their agreement with baseline data documenting the time he was losing with his daughters on a day-by-day basis and on a yearly basis.

5. Asking for mediation.

6. Asking for a court date.

7. Going to court.

In this case Randy and his lawyer decided against mediation because Lenore was negotiating in bad faith. However, when they asked
for a court date, Lenore started complying with the agreement. The
true value of understanding muscle level is that you will tend to escalate consciously and proactively rather than unconsciously and reactively. This can help you avoid the common mistakes of either too
much or too little muscle level.

2.5 Your opening statement

Your opening statement is critical to the success of your negotiation
for two reasons. First, your opening statement sets the tone for the
entire negotiation.

Second, in my opinion, 90 percent of the way a negotiation turns
out depends on how it begins. It is for these reasons that both parties
should prepare a good opening statement.

A large part of developing a good opening statement is knowing
the difference between foreground and background. To illustrate this,
picture in your mind's eye a sailboat on the water. In this case, the
sailboat is the foreground and the water is the background. Part of developing a good opening statement is knowing exactly what should be
in the foreground and what should be in the background.

For example, imagine saying the following to your ex-spouse: "I really have a problem with your not having the children ready every time
I pick them up [foreground].

Other than that, I think we are doing a good job of parenting our
children [background]."How would you respond if your ex-spouse ap-
proached you like that?

Conversely, if your ex-spouse said, "Although this transition has
been tough on all of us, I think we are to be congratulated for being
able to parent as effectively as we have [foreground]. I would like to
come to a better understanding on how we can handle pick-ups from
each other's apartments [background]." No doubt, in most cases an ex-
spouse would respond more favorably to the latter than to the former
because that opening statement puts the working relationship with

your ex-spouse in the foreground and the issue of "how punctual is punctual?" in the background.

In summary, what you choose to put in the foreground and the background and the specific and precise language that you use will go a long way to set the tone of that negotiation. The reason that both parties want to carefully prepare their opening statements is that if the other party opens with an opening statement that sets a poor tone, you can then use your opening statement to set a better tone.

An example of a good opening statement for a couple that is in the process of separating and divorcing is:

> *We are here today to see if we can develop options that will help us maximize our assets and minimize the costs associated with our divorce. At the same time, we will work on developing a shared parenting agreement that is fair and equitable to both the parents and to the children.*

Preparation is key to negotiating success. Knowing what you want out of the process and identifying those points on which you've set your sights is an empowering experience. Walking away from the negotiating table satisfied is a result of hours of work and research; time well spent for your and your children's future.

However, in spite of their best intentions, divorcing or separating individuals often don't use or apply what they have learned in other settings and therefore do not negotiate as effectively and efficiently with their ex-spouses as they could or should.

Now that you better understand the elements that make up the negotiation process, we need to look at the stages that most people must pass through to come to accept the end of their marriage and the stages of the negotiation process in Chapter 4.

4
Understand the Stages

Negotiating a separation or divorce and dismantling a household are hard enough tasks on their own, but most people are going through a grieving process at the same time. The end of a marriage often triggers feelings which can interfere with people's ability to be objective and communicate in productive ways, thus hampering the negotiation process. During the ending of a relationship it is common that the spouses/partners move through the five stages of grief first documented by Elisabeth Kubler-Ross in her groundbreaking research on death and dying.

Understanding the stages of grieving will help you to decide when is a good time to negotiate and to identify the underlying dynamics that affect most couples negotiating a separation or divorce.

1. The Five Stages

Kubler-Ross documented that there are five psychological stages that a person moves through to come to terms with the death of a loved one. Similarly, there are five stages that a person must move through to come to terms with the end of their marriage. Because understanding these stages is so critical to the negotiating process, these stages will be described in detail. The five stages that Kubler-Ross documented are denial, anger, bargaining, depression, and acceptance.

1.1 Denial

In the denial phase of ending a relationship, people often have a great deal of difficulty admitting to themselves — let alone anyone else — that the marriage is in great difficulty. However, once the point is reached when it becomes abundantly clear that there is something radically wrong, enough hurtful words are said, or the lack of psychological support is abundantly clear, people cannot deny the obvious any longer. This is when the grieving process shifts to the second stage.

1.2 Anger

Kubler-Ross states that "when the first stage of denial cannot be maintained any longer, it is replaced by feelings of anger, rage, envy and resentment." Divorcing and separating couples enter this stage where most of what they feel is anger, rage, envy, and resentment. This is a very understandable reaction; one or both partners feel they are losing a shared past history in which they had, in many cases, heavily invested, as well as the future that they dreamed about. In addition, they will lose at least some of their material possessions and a friendship/family network that will for the most part side with one person or the other. There can also be feelings of envy over other couples who have been able to make their marriages/relationships work.

People going through a divorce or separation will sometimes lash out inappropriately, and sometimes almost randomly, at those people around them whom they will ultimately need for support. This misplaced anger can strain relationships and can estrange family, friends, and associates. During this stage, things can and do get very unpredictable. One minute, ex-spouses are very nice and civil to each other. They may even feel closer to each other than they have for a long time because they both share the same sense of loss regarding the ending of the marriage. They may even wonder if they can work it out. And then, the next minute they are back in the throes of feeling hurt, angry, and betrayed.

1.3 Bargaining

In this stage the couple starts bargaining in earnest to see if they can save the relationship. They may take a long-wanted vacation, see a marriage counselor, buy a new house, have a baby, try a trial separation, or some combination of all of the above in an attempt to make the relationship work. If it becomes obvious that none of the above will work, couples often enter the fourth stage: depression.

1.4 Depression

Kubler-Ross talks about two types of depression. The first type of depression is reactive depression. Reactive depression has to do with feelings of loss: loss of a shared past, future dreams, a sense of family and belonging, friends, position, and/or loss of a role. The second type of depression, preparatory depression, prepares us to accept the loss and facilitate a state of acceptance so that we can move on.

Most people go through a stage of depression and intense sadness when they experience a marital breakdown, even if they initiated the separation. And just like when we have lost a loved one, there is often a great deal of support for the person for the first few months. However, research shows that when a spouse has died, it usually takes at least two years to begin to accept the loss and move forward. It often takes the same amount of time to deal with the loss of a marriage. Having a strong support network helps, as does seeking qualified professional help.

Sometimes depression is hard to diagnose and even family physicians miss it, particularly in men. Therefore it is up to you to learn the symptoms by checking with your neighborhood mental health association and with your physician.

1.5 Acceptance

If a patient has had enough time (i.e., is not dealing with a sudden, unexpected death) and has been given some help in working thorough the previously described states, he or she will reach a stage during which he or she is neither depressed nor angry about his fate ... and he will contemplate the end of the process with a certain degree of quiet expectation.

In coping with any type of loss there are three levels of acceptance: accepting, accepting that you have accepted, and then accepting that you have accepted that you have accepted.

When I got the call telling me that my father had died of lung cancer, I thought I was prepared to accept my loss. This was his second bout with lung cancer and the last time I saw him, I knew he did not have long to live. Although I knew I would not see him again on this earth, for the next three months I had the strongest urge to call him on the phone. I could feel my hand wanting to reach out and start dialing his phone number. I was at level one acceptance. I could accept his death intellectually, but was having a much harder time accepting his death emotionally. After six months, I started moving into level two acceptance. I began to accept his death emotionally with the exception of one time of the year: Christmas morning.

In my family of origin and in my wife's family of origin, Christmas presents were opened in the morning. However, my wife's tradition was to open the presents in slow motion; only one person could open a present at a time. You had to very carefully open the present to save the wrapping paper so you could reuse it. In my family, we opened our presents in fast forward. The problem was that Christmas morning was when I most missed my dad, so I wanted Christmas morning over as quickly as possible. While my wife and in-laws were stuck in slow motion, I had the garbage bag out trying to get through the process as quickly as possible. I was solidly in level two acceptance.

Three years later, after my daughter was born, I was no longer in a hurry to get through Christmas morning. Part of the reason for this is the passing of time and that she has the same gentle spirit that my father had. I was now solidly in level three acceptance.

As with a death, there are three levels of acceptance that we all must go through when we become divorced because becoming divorced is not just an intellectual adjustment for most of us, it is also an emotional adjustment. And sadly, there are some people who never get to level three. They never can fully accept that they are divorced and in some cases prefer to have a very bad relationship with their ex-spouse rather than no relationship at all. Other separating and/or divorcing people, given that they have the ability and the support, will learn to accept that their marriage or the relationship is over. It is at this point that they will be able to start moving ahead with their lives because they are able to accept the divorce/separation as a fact of life both intellectually and emotionally.

The truth of the matter is that we do not move through these stages in a lock-step fashion. It is true that we can be in acceptance this morning, and move back into anger and/or depression this afternoon. It is also true that one spouse can be in acceptance while the other is in anger, or vice versa, depending on the day.

It is also true that not everyone moves through all stages at the same speed. There are people who may get stuck in, or have prolonged stays, in one stage or another. Likewise, it is common to vacillate between two or more stages and it is very helpful to realize that this type of vacillation is normal. Grieving and moving forward is neither a simple nor a linear process. However, having a basic understanding of the stages can help you make better decisions about when to negotiate and when not to.

Negotiations over children's scheduling will go much better when both parties are in the stage of acceptance than if one party is in acceptance and the other is in anger or depression.

Just as there are predictable psychological stages that one must pass through to come to terms with and to accept the end of a marriage, there are three predictable stages in the negotiation process.

2. The Three Stages of the Negotiation Process

In their insightful book, *The Practical Negotiator*, (Yale University Press, 1983) Zartman and Berman define negotiations as " ... a process in which divergent values are combined into an agreed decision, and it is based on the idea that there are appropriate stages, sequences, behaviors, and tactics that can be identified and used to improve the conduct of negotiations and better the chances of success." Master negotiators have an intuitive understanding of these stages and of the timing to complete the work required of each stage before going on to the next. By better understanding Zartman and Berman's stages, you will better master the negotiation process. The three stages of the negotiation process are:

- The agreeing to negotiate stage.

- The formula stage.

- The detail stage.

2.1 The agreeing to negotiate stage

In the first stage, the ex-spouses must listen carefully to each other's stories, and to the issues and interests that are behind those stories. They must decide whether negotiation is the preferred method to best meet their needs, and whether there is enough trust, common ground, and goodwill/good faith to enter into negotiations. Alternatively, they may decide that they need the services of a mediator. The mediator will act as the guardian of the process and at times it may be best for the ex-spouses to speak to the mediator rather than each other. Mediation will be covered in much more detail in Chapter 9.

The ex-spouses should also take into account the transaction costs for being in a negotiation. These are the time and effort — sweat equity

— that one invests in the negotiation. Transaction costs are always a part of the negotiation equation and must be factored into the decision to negotiate. It is then necessary to compare the transaction costs for being in a negotiation with the costs of not being in a negotiation. The costs of not negotiating could be the public relations costs of appearing to be intransigent, increased hostility, and prohibitive court costs. Consider divorcing parents who find that the costs of slugging it out in court and paying lawyers' fees for every letter sent become so costly to both parties that they become willing to settle their differences through the process of negotiation and/or mediation. Likewise, in many cases, the cost of continuing to fight and keeping one's life on hold become untenable for all of the parties. They have now entered a mutually hurting stalemate (Worst Alternative To a Negotiated Agreement or WATNA) and the process of negotiation is much more likely to take place.

2.2 The formula stage

When I read Zartman and Berman's formula stage, it was like a light came on. Developing agreed-upon principles and/or formulas frequently accelerates the negotiation process.

Principles/formulas are agreed-upon guidelines for present and future behaviors. An example of a simple formula is that my son helps prepare dinner on even-numbered days and my daughter helps prepare dinner on odd-numbered days (with some sort of fairness worked in for months with odd numbers of days). The agreed-upon formula helps to prevent the problems associated with fairness issues of whose turn it is and who has done the most and/or the least amount of work around the house. Developing formulas is something that most of us do intuitively. However, by making this process conscious, we can do it more frequently, which will help us to negotiate more successfully.

Let me give several separating/divorcing examples of formulas. Dad has the children on Sunday, Monday, and Tuesday nights, and Mom has the children on Wednesday, Thursday, and Friday nights, with Saturday night being negotiable. Mom has the children for Christmas on even-numbered years and Dad has the children for Christmas on odd-numbered years. Mom has the children in odd-numbered months and Dad had the children in even-numbered months. There are an infinite number of possibilities; we just need to tap into a different way of thinking about what is possible. I can say that from interviewing as many separated and divorced couples as I did, I got the sense that there are a far greater number of possibilities than I had ever imagined.

The best negotiators come to the table with several possible formulas and are flexible in changing the formulas. They are also able to adapt and integrate all or some aspects of the formulas proposed by their ex-spouses. Formulas must be flexible so that they can be changed and/or improved as circumstances change over time, as the following example of Deborah and Scott illustrates.

One of the first negotiations we had to tackle is who has the children when. Some of these negotiations were very easy. Scott has the children on his birthday, and Deborah has them on her birthday. Other negotiations were more complex and took a lot more effort and more time to resolve. Deborah and Scott started out with two-day rotations. This worked at first because they were both used to seeing the children every day and enjoyed being actively involved in their lives. On the other hand, it was disruptive to change homes every two days. The children just got used to being with one parent and then they had to change. It also meant that there were more times when they were in one house and the things that they needed were in another. Scott and Deborah then changed to a schedule of Scott having the children Sunday, Monday, and Tuesday nights, Deborah having the children Wednesday, Thursday and Friday nights, with Saturday nights negotiable depending on what worked out best for everyone's schedule. There was flexibility built into the system, but the three-day rotations worked extremely well for them when the children were in elementary school, and once they arrived at this formula, things got to be much easier for everyone.

The next major negotiation was for summer holidays. This was a more contentious negotiation. Deborah and Scott negotiated that Deborah would have first choice of summer vacation dates during even-numbered years and Scott would have first choice during odd-numbered years. The next major negotiation after that was for Christmas and Easter holidays. Scott and Deborah eventually worked out a formula that was mutually satisfactory for those times as well. On even-numbered years, Scott would have the children Christmas Eve and Christmas morning and Deborah would have the children over for Christmas dinner. For odd-numbered years it would be reversed with Deborah having the children for Christmas Eve and Christmas morning and Scott having the children at his house for Christmas dinner.

Master negotiators are aware of the importance of developing mutually agreed-upon principles and/or formulas. Once we become aware of how helpful they can be in reaching successful solutions, we can use the idea of developing formulas more consciously and systematically. Finding formulas that work is a matter of skill, intuition, experience, trial and error, and asking others what worked for them. The necessity to work out a feasible formula holds true in all types of negotiations from financial, to time management or any of the myriad negotiations separating and divorcing partners must face. The following exercises have been designed to help you develop a better sense of this skill.

Exercise 4
Formulas

Think back over three successful negotiations you and your ex-spouse have been in. Briefly describe one situation or issue and write down the principle/formula that was instrumental in helping to resolve the problem or conflict that brought you to the table in the first place.

1. The situation or issue was?

   _____

   _____

   The principle/formula we used to help resolve the situation was:

   _____

   _____

2. Another situation or issue was?

   _____

   _____

   The principle/formula we used to help resolve the situation was:

   _____

   _____

3. A third situation or issue was?

   _____

   _____

   The principle/formula we used to help resolve the situation was:

   _____

   _____

Exercise 4 — Continued

4. What have you learned from analyzing these three principles/ formulas?

   _____

   _____

5. What, if anything, would you do differently in the future?

   _____

   _____

Exercise 5
Observations from Others

Talk to several other people that are going or have gone through a divorce or separation. Ask them whether they use the concept of formulas to negotiate more effectively. Write down three observations that can help you negotiate more effectively.

1.

2.

3.

Exercise 6
Possible Formulas for Next Negotiation

Think of a current or upcoming negotiation that you and your ex-spouse are or will be involved in. To begin your preparations as early as possible, list possible formulas that you will bring to the table for that particular negotiation. Next, every time you think of a new formula that could aid in the negotiation process, add that formula to your list. Lastly, ask a trusted friend or advisor for ideas about creative formulas that might help resolve the particular issue that you will be negotiating.

1.

2.

3.

Last, no one likes to have formulas, no matter how good, imposed upon them. A formula imposed becomes a formula opposed. For example, one of the persons I interviewed named Charlotte stated that, "Even when my ex-husband David did have a good idea, I often opposed it because when we were married he was such a control freak."

3. The Detail Phase

Working out the details of the negotiation formula verifies the effectiveness of the formula in the nitty-gritty of the real world. If the formula works as it is being applied, it helps the parties trust that the agreement they are working on is in fact a valid agreement. Note that hostility and anger are to be expected during this stage. There is a big difference between an agreement in principle and actually working out that agreement in detail. You may find that your formula, which worked perfectly in the abstract, does not work so well in actual practice, and that it has to be modified or scrapped entirely and a new formula developed that better meets the interests of all of the parties. It is in this details phase that real sacrifices and concessions have to be made. These sacrifices and concessions are much more painful in reality than in the abstract. For all of the above reasons, the old adage, "the devil is in the details," takes on special meaning.

Zartman and Berman state in their book, "The settlement of details is a formula's only test and can be accomplished only on a trial and error basis. There are times when speedy agreement on a formula is followed by a long and arduous search for agreement on details."

Take, for example, a divorcing husband and wife who make an agreement (develop a formula) to split all of the household items 50/50, with both parties keeping the furniture that they had before they were married. The development of this formula was relatively easy. The details of who actually gets which piece of furniture, CD, video, picture album, kitchen appliance, spice, or dishware is usually much slower, more complicated, and likely to engender more heated debate and hostility than the devising of the formula. Although most readers will agree with the above, it is also true that the process would be much more arduous and difficult without a formula.

No matter how careful the parties are in developing their formulas, there will be times when the details take over and the couple has to legitimately decide what to do. For example, take Nancy and Bert.

Nancy and Bert had decided that Nancy would have first choice of times for summer vacation during even-numbered years and Bert would have first choice for summer vacation time during odd-numbered years. This arrangement worked very well for five years. In year six, a major conflict arose.

Year six was an even-numbered year, and as per their agreement, Nancy had first choice. Nancy had scrimped and saved for five years to have enough money so she and the children could go to Disney World. The plane tickets had been purchased in January and they were going to Disney World from August 26 to 31. Since this year was her time to have the children first, she hadn't yet told Bert when they were going, when she received an upsetting telephone call from Bert in February.

Bert wanted to take the children to a family reunion that was being scheduled from August 28 to 30 of that year in Chicago. Realizing that there was a conflict with Nancy's plans, Bert phoned his cousin, who was one of the main organizers, to see if the family reunion could be rescheduled. His cousin told him that the organizing committee had already given a non-refundable deposit on the hotel, they had already received four requests to change the date, all of which conflicted, and that the majority of the family could come on August 28, so he was sorry but he could not change the date at this point.

Bert then got back on the phone with Nancy and explained the importance of being able to attend their family reunion and the fact that his parents were getting on in age and might not be around for the next one. Nancy then explained that her airline tickets were also non-refundable and that she had already asked for and had been given the last week in August as her vacation time from work.

At this point both Nancy and Bert realized that they had a difficult problem to solve, that both parties' interests were legitimate, and that they would have to work to negotiate a successful outcome to their dilemma. In the end, Bert paid Nancy's fees to change her reservations and Nancy and the children rescheduled their trip to Disney World. Both parties felt that this arrangement was as fair as possible under the circumstances. They also vowed to keep each other better informed, knowing that similar issues would crop up again on both sides. However, since the problem was worked out so well, there was both goodwill in the bank and a mental model of a successful negotiation in the past, which would make similar future negotiations easier. Lastly, they demonstrated a positive model for resolving conflict for their children.

3.1 Repeat and write down the details

Repeating the details and writing them down are proven methods in preventing conflicts and/or helping to prevent conflict escalation. For example, my ex-wife and I had agreed that I would have the children the weekend of August 25. The children had spent the previous week with my ex-wife's parents. Being a strong believer in the importance of family, I supported this completely.

That year, the week with their grandparents came after two weeks at camp and two weeks' summer vacation with their mother, which meant I hadn't seen the children for four weeks. As I was anxious to see the children, I offered to pick the children up at their grandparents' house on Friday night. My ex-wife said that she did not want to rush home after dinner. I said "OK," thinking I would pick the children up first thing Saturday and then we would head down to our cottage. I got up early Saturday morning and called my ex-wife at her house because I got the feeling that she had spent the night at her parents'. There was no answer, so I suspected that my hunch was right.

I called my ex-wife at her parents'. Her mother said she was over at her sister's. I called her sister. My ex said that she told me that she was coming home early Saturday morning. We both had different recollections as to what our agreement had been. We both realized that there was no use getting angry or upset. We had to come up with a method that would prevent this type of misunderstanding from happening in the future.

We came up with two proposals so we could better document our agreements. One proposal was that we could email a copy of our agreements back and forth, that way each party would know exactly what the agreement was. The other was that we could repeat the agreement and write down the times that the children would be with each of us in our daily planners. The latter seemed to be the most feasible because we would not have to have access to a computer at the time we were making our agreements. Our new procedure of repeating our agreements and writing them in our daily planners significantly decreased the number of misunderstandings we had. Of course, more modern ex-spouses also have the choice of keeping track of their agreements on their smart phones.

Putting all major agreements regarding parenting into a joint parenting agreement helps to clarify both parties' understanding, will help to reduce conflicts about who said what, and demonstrates that there was enough goodwill to come to an agreement which will help to make any changes and/or future negotiations easier, because the parents can see how they have been able to come to important agreements in the past.

An example of a shared parenting agreement where there is low level of conflict between the parents follows. Please note that the agreement starts with an agreement of the principles on which the agreement is reached. It then covers specific agreements in more detail. More specifically it covers scheduling, conflict resolution, and the process on how to renew or change the agreement, as new issues arise.

Sample 2
Dale and Roy's Parenting Agreement

We will work to find solutions that are creative to best meet the needs of the children and parents alike. Therefore this agreement is an agreement in principle. The agreement can be signed or unsigned. The goal of the agreement is to balance structure and flexibility to best meet the needs and desires of the parents and children alike.

Right of First Refusal: If either party cannot take the children on his or her specified and agreed-upon dates, the other party will have the right of first refusal to take the children before going to an outside party.

In principle, we agree to a week-on and a week-off schedule. Both parties will be as flexible as possible in making this schedule work. Roy will make every effort to book his travel time during his week off. If that is not possible, Roy and Dale will see if we can change dates. If it is not possible, Roy is responsible for finding childcare for the children and vice versa.

When the children are with Roy, he will be responsible for taking the children and their belongings to Dale's around 4:00 p.m. on alternating Sundays. When the children are with Dale, she will be responsible for taking the children and their belongings to Roy around 4:00 p.m.

on alternating Sundays. Any items left behind will be the responsibility of the parent of the house where the children traveled from, and/or it will be the responsibility of the children, and not the responsibility of the parent the children have traveled to.

Specific Dates: Christmas Eve will be spent at Roy's. Christmas day until approximately 2:00 p.m. will be spent at Dale's. Otherwise the Christmas holiday will be split evenly between the parent's homes.

Roy will have the children on his birthday and on Father's Day. Dale will have the children on her birthday and on Mother's Day. Dale will have first choice of summer holidays with the children in even-numbered years and Roy will have first choice of summer holidays with the children in odd-numbered years.

Dale will have the children for Thanksgiving in even-numbered years and Labor Day weekend on odd numbered years. Roy will have the children for Thanksgiving in odd numbered years and Labor Day weekend on even-numbered years. Easter will be shared by Dale and Roy in amanner that is mutually acceptable and March Break will be shared in a manner that works best for all parties.

Daniel and Tina's Birthdays: If either child wants to have a birthday party, it will be the responsibility of one parent to plan and host the party one year and the other party to plan and host the party the following year.

School Supplies: Roy will buy the children's school supplies in odd-numbered years and Dale will buy the children's school supplies in even-numbered years.

This agreement can be changed at any time with the mutual consent of all pertinent parties. If for any reason, agreement cannot be reached, the parties agree to seek the help of a qualified mediator. Otherwise, this agreement will be in effect until December 31st of every year at which time the parties will review it and accept it as it stands for the coming year, or change it, as long as the changes are agreed to by all of the parties concerned.

If there is a high degree of conflict between the parties, then the shared parenting agreement has to be much more specific, and depending on the degree of conflict, may need to be spelled out in minute detail. For example, the agreement may need to state who the children's dentist is, the fact that the parents will make alternate trips with the children to the dentist, and that the person who took the children to the dentist will be responsible for paying that amount of the bill that each parent's dental plan does not cover, with the total amount spent on dental bills to be reconciled by June 30 and December 31 of each year. Conversely, if one parent has a dental plan and the other parent does not have a dental plan, then arrangements can be made for the parent without a dental plan to pay a similar amount of another activity such as dance class or a specific sporting activity.

To find out more about how to develop an effective parenting agreement where there is a moderate to high level of conflict between the parents, I encourage you to read a very helpful book by Philip M. Stahl entitled *Parenting After Divorce: A Guide to Resolving Conflicts and Meeting Your Children's Needs* (Impact Publishers, 2007).

Lastly, Isolina Ricci, PhD, the author of *Mom's House, Dad's House: Making Two Homes for Your Child* (Touchstone, 1997), makes a very interesting recommendation as to how parents can use their parenting agreements. Ricci recommends that the parents consider making a parenting agreement that the children can read. As such, the agreement should be written using fair language such as "shared parenting agreement" rather than "custody." She also recommends that if the child or children are old enough, they should be able to see the agreement because a well-written agreement will show the children that their parents want to be cooperative, fair, and have the best interests of the children at heart. Ricci also points out that: "The simplicity of an agreement written in everyday terms, with the intent and details of decisions clearly spelled out, helps children as well as parents to understand and appreciate what to expect and what will be expected of them. Since the document is about what will happen to your children, it stands to reason that children should have the right to read it and understand what it means to them."

However, where this is a moderate to high degree of conflict between the parents, showing children the joint parenting agreement may not be in the children's best interests. The decision to show or not to show the shared parenting agreement should be in both the parent's and the children's best interests. If you are not sure whether to show or not show the agreement to your children, consider asking a child development expert his or her opinion and remember that this expert may need to meet and talk with your children before giving his or her professional opinion.

Once you have ground rules and tools in place, you will be ready to move on to identifying your negotiating style in the next chapter. Knowing your style is critical because it will pervade every aspect of your negotiations.

5

Make Your Negotiating Style Work for You, Not Against You

No matter how well-prepared or well-intentioned you may be when entering a negotiation, it can all fall apart if negotiating styles — that is, your own and your ex-spouse's — are overlooked. As Maggie's story illustrates, if she had not had the foresight to identify her and her ex-husband's style, not only the negotiations, but the ultimate outcome for Maggie, her ex-husband, and their daughter, would have been much different. Maggie said:

> We had a non-traditional marriage in that both of us were in the military. We separated when our daughter, Noelle, was eight months old and today she is 16 years old. At the time my ex-husband, Ashley, was posted to a different city than I was and that made a difficult marriage even more difficult. Right from the start, Ashley was negotiating in bad faith. He tried to get me for abandonment of our daughter when I left the marriage because I had left some of our things in the house. However, in the end, we were awarded joint custody.
>
> After we separated, due to training and some overseas posting, we shared childcare 50/50, but the time periods that worked best for our military careers was six-months-on, six-months-off, and this lasted until Noelle was of school age.

Then I received a very isolated six-month posting in the Arctic. Since it could be very difficult for anyone to get a hold of me, I was advised by my lawyer to sign the legal responsibility for Noelle's medical day-to-day care over to Ashley. This made perfect sense to me, because if there were a medical emergency, and no one could get a hold of me, I did not want to put Noelle at risk.

What I didn't anticipate when I returned from my six-month posting, was that Ashley would use my signing over the medical day-to-day care responsibility over to him to his trying to get sole custody. I had signed that agreement in good faith, and he used it against me. At first I only had visitation on Tuesday nights and every second weekend, and this was extraordinarily difficult for me. It felt like he had taken my daughter away from me.

We then had a battle across three states with five different sets of lawyers trying to get things settled. It was brutal. In the end, I was given day-to-day care of Noelle, and Ashley, who lives on the other side of the country, has a one-month visitation every summer.

The best advice I could give anyone who has to deal with someone who negotiates in bad faith is to get yourself a very good lawyer, and if you don't like your lawyer, search around until you find someone in whom you have confidence and with whom you are comfortable. This is especially true when you are in a crisis as I was when Ashley tried to get sole custody based on an agreement that I made in good faith. In fact, when you are in a crisis like I was I needed a social worker/therapist/lawyer combination.

Another issue I had to deal with was child support. One night Ashley called and said he wasn't going to pay child support. I told him that was something he would have to work out with the courts and not with me. Now all his payments have to be registered with Family Court.

B.M.: How did you have the self control not to get emotionally hooked when he said that he was going to stop sending the child support payments?

M: It was an adult issue and it had to be settled between the adults. If he was not going to act like an adult, then he would have to interface with the courts, not me. I also did it this way because I had to separate adult issues from child issues. So I never said we can't do this or that because he didn't send the money.

In the end, I had no idea of how painful or expensive those years would be, especially when I only had visitation rights on Tuesday nights and every other weekend. In the end, it would have been cheaper to hire a hitman — just kidding.

I must admit that, in hindsight, all of this has taught me a great deal about value differences. We were married when I was 19 and he was in his early 20s. As we grew older our value differences were just too great to sustain the marriage, and that was a good thing. There are options in life and he is not one of the options I want to have in my life, except to the extent that he is and can be a good father to Noelle. In the end, I turned out to be more of a free spirit, someone who believes strongly in "joie de vivre" and at the same time, someone who has a strong sense of responsibility.

B.M.: Can you give me a specific example?

M: Education was not a goal in his life. If Noelle had lived with Ashley, she wouldn't have the same value system that she has today. I have tried to teach Noelle to create options in her life and then she can decide. I wanted her to recognize that she can be the best that she can be. I wanted her to learn how to push the boundaries; that not all trees have to be green. I also keep my eyes on my ultimate goal. Sometimes you have to let time prove things wrong. Noelle was always my first concern. I didn't want her to become a screwed-up teenager, so I kept her out of our adult conflicts. I knew time would take me through this and that nothing stays constant. I could not control how he treated me; I could control how it impacted me. I also knew that I didn't want to be the single embittered mother. I couldn't allow myself to be a victim.

He felt that I destroyed his world, because I caught him cheating. I told him to deal with it because he was the one who had the affair. He would then tell Noelle that I left him and I left her. This was patently not true so I would always keep it very simple by telling him that he was the one I left.

I am proud of the fact that I am [an]independent single mother. I have my mother and two sisters for support, and they are all excellent with Noelle. I also have some very good male friends. So I think that to a certain extent, I have been able to be a role model for Noelle. She has turned out very well. She plays tennis, goes to the gym to work out, does kickboxing, is a big music buff, and is an excellent student.

One summer he said he couldn't afford to bring Noelle out because he and his new family were moving. It was presented as a "fait accompli" that was non-negotiable.

Although this violated the divorce agreement and I both wanted and needed a break from the responsibilities of parenting, I didn't push it, because I didn't want Noelle to go out and feel unwanted, or to listen to Ashley complain about me. It also reinforced my belief that, at heart, he is a very selfish man and now that I am completely out of his life, that's his problem and I would not make it mine. It is a complex balancing act of all of those dynamics.

Today, Noelle and Ashley have a good father/daughter relationship. I could tell her some of the things that I have told you, but it would severely damage or destroy the relationship she has with her father. Throughout this whole ordeal, I was very clear on which problems are adult problems and which problems are child problems. My problems with my ex-husband and his betrayal of trust were adult problems and will probably always be so. It is important to me that Noelle has a good relationship with both of her parents.

From doing the interviews for this book, I have found that there are some amazing people who have learned to act in responsible, mature, and flexible manners, even when their ex-spouses did not. They learned how to negotiate with dignity, maturity, and respect because it was in everyone's best interests to do so. One of the reasons that they could negotiate well was that they understood the importance of understanding their ex-spouse's styles and the importance of controlling the style with which they chose to negotiate.

To help you learn more about the importance of negotiating style, the following sections cover six topics that are central to understanding negotiating style as a whole.

1. Understanding Your Negotiating Style

Your style and that of your ex-spouse is critically important because it pervades every aspect of your negotiations. The best way to understand this is through the following analogy. Imagine you want to move a large rock and no one is around to help. You push and push on the rock, you dig out the area in front of the rock, but after a few minutes, it becomes obvious that it is an impossible situation - you can't move the rock. One choice is to give up. A better choice is to use leverage. You find a two-by-four board and wedge it in between the large rock and a smaller rock (see Figure 3). You are now able to easily move what used to be an immovable object.

Figure 3: The Importance of Knowing Your Negotiating Style

The "lever" in Figure 3 is analogous to our negotiating style, the large rock represents the negotiation, and the result or outcome of the negotiation is determined by the direction the rock is moving in. In other words, if we control our style (the lever), we have better control over the negotiation (the large rock), and hence we have better control over the outcome of the negotiation (moving the rock). Therefore, it is imperative that we know what our negotiation style is and how to make it work for us rather than against us.

2. Understanding Your Ex-Spouse's/ Ex-Partner's Negotiation Style

Please note that I use the word "partner," not "opponent" or "adversary." This is a vital distinction for three reasons. First, if we view someone as an adversary or opponent, and if that person subsequently does something that is cooperative, we run the risk of not even seeing it and/or of discounting it because that behavior does not fit with the way we have chosen to view the situation and/or the other party. In other words, we have to be vigilant both to create opportunities for cooperation and to clearly see and react positively to them when they are presented to us.

Second, if we view the other party as our partner, we can look carefully as to how he or she uses language to phrase his or her argument. We can also look for the underlying values, metaphors, and analogies that are important to the other party. By listening to how the other person uses language, values, metaphors, and analogies, we can then make our points in his or her language, values, metaphors, and analogies; and the result is that your ex-spouse is more likely to be able to hear what you have to say. The skill of listening to the other party's language, values, metaphors, and analogies is a method of applying Stephen Covey's sage advice "Seek first to understand and then seek to be understood."(From *The 7 Habits of Highly Effective People* (Simon & Schuster, 1989).

Third, there are times when we have to modify our preferred negotiation style to match the other party's style in order to get the other party to take us seriously. For example, if your ex-spouse is a hard bargainer, you may need to be phenomenally assertive in order for him/her to treat you with any respect and credibility because that is the only style that he/she understands.

For example, Mary has sole custody of their son, Aaron. Her ex-husband, Jim, has visitation rights every Wednesday night and every other weekend. Jim had always been on time and had always shown up to get Aaron until Mary started dating Steve. Thereafter, Jim would often show up late or not at all, leaving Mary to deal with the fallout of a distraught four-year-old: "Where is my Daddy? I want my Daddy," and an unhappy Steve because Mary and Steve couldn't follow through on their plans for a night out.

Mary prefers to negotiate collaboratively; however in this situation, being collaborative and discussing the matter only resulted in promises to do better next time that were never kept, and Mary, Aaron, and Steve were all becoming increasingly frustrated. Finally they agreed on a grace period of half an hour. Jim was late as usual, but in this case, Mary had prearranged to drop Aaron off at his regular babysitter. When Mary got home she received a telephone call from a very furious Jim. Mary responded that if Jim kept his agreements it would not interfere with his ability to be with his son. At the same time, she would not allow her social life to be held hostage. By adjusting her negotiating style, Mary was able to solve the problem of Jim's tardiness.

3. The Effectiveness of the Various Styles

One of the very best sources of scientific information on negotiation style is the research conducted by Gerald R. Williams (*Negotiation: Strategies for Mutual Gain*, Sage Publications) of the Faculty of Law at Brigham Young University. The main goal of this study was to identify the characteristics of highly effective negotiators. He found that there were three primary negotiating styles. The first style is the cooperative style or your quintessential "win-win" negotiator. The second style is your competitive negotiator or your quintessential "win as much as you can [win-lose]" negotiator. The third was labelled "No Pattern." Although some people have mixed styles, it is important to look at the pure forms first, and to make the more subtle distinctions later.

It is also important to note that Williams determined that there were three subcategories for each style: effective, average, and ineffective. Therefore, knowing that you have a cooperative style is not sufficient, you need to know if you use that style effectively, ineffectively, or as the average person does. For example, ineffective cooperatives are gullible and naïve, and subsequently are frequently taken advantage of.

We must also learn the important distinctions between cooperative negotiators and competitive negotiators if we are to negotiate effectively with people who have a style that is different from our own preferred style. The difference between these styles and the characteristics shared by both types of effective negotiators are summarized in Table 2.

Table 2
Styles of Effective Cooperative and Competitive Negotiators

Cooperative Objectives	Competitive Objectives
1. Conduct self ethically.	1. Maximize the settlement for themselves.
2. Maximize settlement.	
3. Get a fair settlement.	2. Win the arguments.
	3. Outdo or outmaneuver opponent.

Cooperative Traits	Competitive Traits
1. Trustworthy, ethical, fair.	1. Dominating, forceful, attacking.
2. Courteous, personable, tactful, sincere.	2. Plans timing and sequence of actions (strategy), rigid, uncooperative.
3. Fair minded.	
4. Realistic opening position.	3. Carefully observes opponent.
5. Accurately evaluates case.	4. Unrealistic opening position.
6. Does not use threats.	5. Clever.
7. Willing to share information.	6. Uses threats.
8. Skilfully probes ex-spouse's interests.	7. Reveals information gradually.
	8. Willing to stretch the facts.

Effective Cooperatives: Cooperatives are quintessential "win-win" negotiators who focus on mutual gains. They are creative problem solvers and want a good outcome where all of the parties can consider that they were treated fairly. They would like all sides to feel good about the outcome, the relationships between the parties and the process used to arrive at that outcome. Effective cooperatives are able to both create and claim value and are flexible. In addition, they are able to use power effectively when necessary. In sum, they are strategically cooperative.

Ineffective Cooperatives: If effective cooperatives are strategically cooperative, ineffective cooperatives are unconditionally cooperative. In other words they are cooperative both when it makes sense to be so but also when it does not. They are consistently too trustful, gullible, naïve and easily taken advantage of, and are known to have "given away the farm." They are also too "gentle, obliging, patient, and forgiving." No matter what their ex-spouse does, they will try to get along. Ineffective cooperatives are not good at claiming value for themselves, and, because they are so trusting and so forgiving, they encourage others to "claim value" against them. Ineffective cooperatives therefore are frequently taken advantage of.

Table 2 — Continued

Effective Competitives: Competitive negotiators are the quintessential "win as much as you can" or "win-lose" negotiators. They want to be the winner and claim most, if not all of the value. Effective competitives come to the table incredibly well prepared and are flexible. This means that although they try to "win" the negotiation by being aggressive and well-prepared, if that strategy turns out not to work because they are dealing with another effective negotiator, no matter what the style of that other negotiator (competitive, cooperative, or no pattern) they have the flexibility and the ability to collaborate and/or compromise, because getting a deal is better than not getting a deal. In other words, although effective competitives place more emphasis on claiming value, they are flexible enough to create value if the situation warrants it. Gerald Williams' research shows that only one out of four people can use the competitive style of negotiation effectively.

Ineffective Competitives: Ineffective competitives use their style solely to intimidate, bully, and bluff their way through the negotiation because they are, in fact, ill-prepared. Ineffective competitives have very little flexibility and when faced with a strategy that is not working, and they tend to maintain or increase the level of aggression. This often results in the negotiation breaking off, the deal remains unmade, and the relationship between the parties is often damaged. Because of their inflexibility they see the world only in terms of opponents. They only know how to claim value and they tend to be poor at seeing the larger picture or seeing out-of-the-box solutions, hence are very poor at creating value. In fact, Williams found that ineffective competitives were so demanding that others typically find them to be obnoxious, and that obnoxious behavior often ends up working against them.

On the outside Mike and Susan looked like an ideal couple. They had been together for 22 years, shared many interests, and were always the life of the party. No one knew it, but Mike and Susan had been going to marriage counselors for a number of years and had made an agreement that they would give themselves one more year's counseling and then try a trial separation if things didn't improve.

In the middle of the year, Susan became suspicious that Mike was having an affair. Unbeknownst to Mike, Susan had the computer skills to find the evidence on Mike's computer. Susan confronted Mike and Mike admitted his affair. Because Mike had always respected Susan so much, he was as devastated by his behavior as she was. Mike felt so guilty, that he let Susan have the majority of their belongings, the majority of the equity they had in their house, and the majority of their savings. But as soon as they reached any settlement, Susan asked for more and Mike usually gave it to her. Now, Mike is in a solid, long-term relationship. His partner is ready to retire and Mike would like to retire with her, only he can't. Mike had previously appeased his guilt by giving in to Susan's every demand. Susan's anger propelled her to keep asking for more. Mike was focused only on his appeasing his guilt and lost complete sight of his long-term security. As this example demonstrates, ineffective cooperatives tend to give away the farm. If you find that you are in a situation where you are being too cooperative, have someone else negotiate on your behalf, or at least use an outside party as a sounding board to help you balance both your short-term and your long-term interests.

* * *

After four years of trying to save their marriage, Eric and Noreen decided to separate and divorce. Unfortunately, the tensions did not lessen; rather they increased as a lengthy custody battle for their six-year-old daughter Danielle ensued. The custody battle lasted two years. In the process Noreen hired and fired three lawyers because they were not aggressive enough. She not only wanted total custody, she wanted to destroy Eric's character in the process by accusing him of sexually assaulting their daughter.

A psychologist was called in to evaluate Danielle. The psychological report cleared Eric of any and all charges. The judge interviewed Danielle in his chambers away from both her parents. In the end the judge awarded joint custody, feeling that Danielle would benefit from a continued relationship with both her parents. However, he did admonish Noreen that she had gone too far in trying to assassinate Eric's character, and that if she continued, it would have adverse consequences. He further told her that her behavior not only did not strengthen her case for sole custody — it weakened it.

I strongly recommend that you consciously learn to recognize both your own style and the styles of the people with whom you negotiate. You also want to learn where your style works for you, where it works against you, and the changes or corrections that you need to make in your style such as increased flexibility, or how to increase your own negotiating power so your style will work for you in an increasingly large number of circumstances. In summary, one of the biggest challenges we need to face is how to negotiate successfully with people who use each of the main negotiation styles. The reason we have to do this consciously is to correct for our natural tendency to assume that all negotiators work from the same set of assumptions we do. These four styles are summarized in Table 3.

Table 3
Characteristics of Effective and Ineffective Negotiators by Style

Cooperative Style: Effective	Competitive Style: Effective
cooperative	warrior
creative problem solvers	willing to fight to the end for beliefs
Cooperative Style: Ineffective	**Competitive Style: Ineffective**
naïve	headstrong
gullible	intolerant
too idealistic	impatient
unsure of self	rigid
lacking in confidence	demanding
too obliging	unreasonable
frequently taken advantage of	uncooperative
easy target	arrogant
soft touch	devious
pushover	conniving
	bluffer
	unwilling to share information
	quarrelsome
	rude
	hostile
	obstructive
	unrealistic
	positional

3.1 Styles negotiating with each other

One way to further examine these patterns is to look at what happens when the various types of negotiators negotiate with each other.

3.1a Effective cooperative negotiating with effective cooperative

Effective cooperative and effective cooperative is a match made in heaven. If the problem has a creative, mutual gain solution, they will find it.

3.1b Effective competitive negotiating with effective competitive

An effective competitive with another effective competitive is a combination where you might expect a brawl. However, since they both understand each other because they speak the same language, they are well-prepared and can see that neither one will back down, and since getting an agreement is better than not getting an agreement and since they know they will have to negotiate with each other in the future, they will eventually collaborate or compromise because as effective negotiators they can see that it is in their best interests to do so.

3.1c Effective cooperative negotiating with effective competitive

The competitive will beat the cooperative every time unless the cooperative is effective. To be effective, the cooperative has to accurately diagnose the negotiating style of the person with whom he or she is negotiating, come to the table impeccably well prepared, have developed a good BATNA, and be able to use power or force effectively. Seeing this, the effective competitive will have the flexibility to negotiate collaboratively and/or to compromise because getting a deal is better than not getting a deal. The effective competitive also knows that at some time in the future, he or she will need to ask for a favor from their effective cooperative counterpart, and developing goodwill in the current negotiation will make it much more likely that a desirable outcome will be able to be negotiated in the future.

Which is the better strategy? And what does all of this research tell us about negotiating? First, we need to know our own primary styles, cooperative or competitive. Second, we need to examine how our styles work with people who use a similar style. Third, and perhaps the most interesting aspect of researching our own negotiating styles' effectiveness will be our comparisons when we negotiate with someone who uses a style different from our preferred style.

For example, if you are a competitive negotiator paired with a cooperative or a cooperative negotiator paired with a competitive, you need to know where your style works and where you need to make changes in the way you negotiate. By accurately identifying your own style of negotiating as well as identifying the style of the person with whom you are negotiating, you are much more likely to negotiate effectively. You are also much more likely to make informed choices during the negotiation process and, therefore, much more likely to negotiate outcomes that are favorable. There is one more piece of information that will help us all negotiate more effectively, and that is understanding the traits that both types of effective, negotiators, whether they be cooperative or competitive, have in common.

- They come to the table incredibly well-prepared.

- They can be flexible when flexibility is warranted.

- They have incredible self-control.

Please note that coming to the table well prepared, having the ability to be appropriately flexible, and having impeccable self-control results in increased self-confidence, and increased self-confidence is one of the most salient hallmarks of effective negotiators.

Learning how to do the above is easier said than done, but I am confident that you can do it if you make a correct diagnosis and come to the table incredibly well-prepared as the examples in this and other chapters point out.

3.1d Dealing effectively with mixed styles

Among the most difficult people to negotiate with are those who use a mixed style, and most people have mixed styles. Stacey asked me how she could more effectively negotiate with her ex-husband Glenn.

> My ex-spouse drives me crazy. I never know from one moment to the next if he will be cooperative or adversarial. He will even mix tactics in the same negotiation. By the end, I don't know whether I am coming or going. As a consequence, I find that I am being nice one minute and am an angry, raving lunatic the next. I am sure that this is, at best, confusing for our children and at worst, we are doing positive damage to their ability to form and sustain relationships in the future. How do I handle this?

This is a difficult adjustment for both Stacey and Glenn and it sounds as if they both are not sure how to act with each other and probably emotionally hook each other.

First, by using the methods outlined in this chapter on how to un-hook their core values, they may be able to settle the issues more effectively. Second, they can analyze both their own and their ex-spouses' negotiating styles over time. The information at the end of this chapter on overly cooperative and overly competitive styles may prove to be very helpful. Third, they can both see a mediator to help them settle specific issues and can hopefully learn a process that will help them deal with issues more effectively in the future (mediation will be covered more thoroughly in the next chapter). Fourth, there may be some issues that they can agree on and there may be other issues that they have to learn how to agree to disagree on. Last, if none of the above work, they will have to learn to accept the fact that some things may never change, but they can learn to mitigate the effects of the undesired behavior. In other words, they learn to change their perspectives through perspective management.

4. Identifying and Controlling Your Shadow Style

The term "shadow style" refers to a more primitive negotiation style that comes into play when we get emotionally hooked and therefore negotiate less well than we could or we should. The following is an excellent example of how we get emotionally hooked.

> When Jack became a father he swore that he would never make his children feel guilty if they did not eat everything on their plates by talking about starving children in other parts of the world. Then one day, when everything that could have gone wrong at work went wrong, and Jack's self-esteem and frustration tolerance level were at an all-time low, he came home from work and the children were at him from the moment he opened the door. He sat down at the dinner table vowing to have a relaxing meal with his family. The children complained about the food, picking at this and trying to hide that, moving more food than they were eating, and then all of a sudden, those very words that Jack swore would never be spoken in his household about the starving children in less fortunate parts of the world passed through his lips.

This scenario graphically illustrates the process of becoming emotionally hooked with a shadow style coming to the forefront. Our shadow styles are even more likely to get hooked when we negotiate with our ex-spouses. The relationship with your ex-spouse can be fraught with unresolved issues from the past as well as the present. You know each other well enough to not only know what the hot buttons are, but also how to press them for maximum advantage. For example, John's preferred style is to be warm, open, and congenial, however when he is overly tired or has very strong feelings about an issue, his shadow style may be quite aggressive and he inappropriately starts acting like Attila the Hun. Our shadow styles can be responsible for breaking off, giving in, or escalating a conflict. It is important not only to improve our primary styles, but also to control our shadow styles.

At this point I would like to give an example that demonstrates how Cora became emotionally hooked in the middle of a negotiation with her ex-husband.

> I was negotiating with my ex-husband about changing from a three-day-on/three-day-off schedule to a week-on and week-off schedule as I felt this would be better for the children now that they were older. Their friends could find them more easily and it would mean fewer moves and therefore fewer adjustments. Although our son had little difficulty adjusting from one house to the other, our daughter did. In fact we both noticed our daughter was in a bad mood whenever she changed houses. It is also true that a week on and a week off would better suit my travel schedule. When I proposed that we make these changes, my ex-husband asked if my schedule worked out exactly so that it would always be a week on and a week off.
>
> I went ballistic! I thought he was needling me. We also had a history of my making proposals, which he would shoot down or say no to, but would not make any proposals himself. The trouble is that I realized that I was overreacting and that my shadow style had taken over, but at the time, I just couldn't help myself.

The first thing I would say to Cora is congratulations on being aware that she was becoming emotionally hooked. Awareness is often the first step in the process of change. The next thing I would say to Cora is to anticipate at least five of her ex-husband's questions and develop rational, non-emotionally hooked responses. For example, in the above case, Cora should be ready to say that the schedule works out perfectly except for two weeks in October when she will be traveling two weeks in a row.

In other words, we do not want to take the behavior — getting emotionally hooked — away from Cora, without giving her a replacement behavior. In this case the replacement behavior is to ask high-yield questions.

Exercise 7
Identifying Your Styles

1. What is my primary negotiating style?

   _____

2. What is my shadow style?

   _____

3. In what types of situations are you most likely to get hooked when negotiating with your ex-spouse?

   _____

4. What skill will you use in place of getting emotionally hooked?

   _____

In summary, our shadow styles come into play when we become emotionally hooked. We lose self-control and negotiate in a manner that is detrimental to the substantive outcome we wish to establish, to the relationships with the other party, or both. In general, when we become emotionally hooked, our shadow style is to become too aggressive, too passive, or too passive-aggressive.

There is one aspect of negotiation style that we have not covered yet, and that is what happens when your negotiation counterpart tries to lull you into complacency by disguising his or her style.

5. Correctly Identifying the Style of Those Who Try to Disguise Their Style

Negotiating with one's ex-spouse can be more difficult still when your ex-spouse has a hidden agenda and/or disguises his or her style, so nowhere is it more important to be well-prepared, to practice diligent self-control, and to identify as thoroughly and as early as possible the negotiation style of the person you will be negotiating with. The following example illustrates the importance of the early understanding of and identification of someone who is trying to disguise his or her negotiating style.

> William's marriage to Martha broke up due to irreconcilable differences. There were two young children involved and Martha had custody of the children, while William had liberal visitation rights. Although it was a very difficult

time for him, William worked hard and was very proactive at maintaining an excellent relationship with his children.

On the surface Martha appeared to be a very cordial, cooperative negotiator. Underneath, she was a competitive/aggressive negotiator. For example, William worked shift work at a local factory. Since he knew what his shifts would be two weeks ahead of time, that is when William and Martha planned the visitation schedule for the upcoming month. It is also important to note that Martha's take-home pay from her work was higher than William's, though, each month William managed to work enough overtime that their incomes were virtually equal. However, where William's shifts were constant, overtime was not. On the surface Martha appeared to be very cooperative when William had to work overtime. Their agreement was that William could make up the time at a later date that was convenient to both parties. Whenever William tried to reschedule the make-up time, it was never a convenient time for Martha.

The lesson learned and reinforced is that master negotiators come to the table incredibly well-prepared, not only on content, but also in their ability to diagnose their counterparts' styles and they have the ability to act and react accordingly.

Finally, William started to keep accurate records on when he had the children and when Martha had the children. He was then able to point out that he only had the children 40 percent of the time and their agreement stipulated that he was to have the children 50 percent of the time, and so if they couldn't come to an agreement he would instruct his lawyer to file for a court date. In the end, William got to see his children 50 percent of the time, but first he had to see that his ex-wife was only cooperative on the surface. Although she agreed to look after the children when he had to work overtime, her shadow style was aggressive in that she did not live up to the spirit of their agreement by letting him make up the time so that each parent would have the children 50 percent of the time.

It is most likely that neither you nor your ex-spouse will be able to disguise your styles for long; however, early identification is still in your best interest as you do not want to set precedents or fall into a pattern of negotiation that will work against you.

6. Inclusiveness

An important element of style that is almost always overlooked in articles, books, and seminars on negotiation is inclusiveness. Inclusiveness has to do with the issue of who should be informed; how much information should be shared; which are individual decisions and which are joint decisions; and when children/teenagers should be included as decision makers and be part of the negotiations.

> Al and Shirley agreed that their daughter Jill could play Tier 2 soccer. Problems arose because Jill turned out to be a very good soccer player and her coach recommended that she play Tier 1 the following summer. In Tier 1 there would be a few more games and practices, but the games would be over a much larger geographical area which would entail even more driving to various soccer fields. Therefore, Shirley told Jill that her answer was no and she would have to play Tier 2 the following summer.

> Al became angry, because he felt disenfranchised as a parent even though he had mixed feelings about Jill playing Tier 1. He felt that Shirley had usurped his position as a co-parent by making a unilateral decision, and Jill was working on Dad to overturn Mom's decision.

> At this point both Mom and Dad were angry at each other and it appeared that there were three adult decision makers in the family rather than two parents and a child. Last, the parents have developed a precedent that will lead to problems in the future, because it is much more likely that Al will get back at Shirley by not including her in some decision in the future. Or, Dad could side with Jill and tell her that she can play Tier 1 because he will do all the driving and wait for World War III to start.

In a case like this, one or both co-parents can call a halt to the proceedings. They can agree that this is a decision that rightly has to be a joint decision. The parents can decide that they need to make a decision first and either agree to go with Tier 1 or Tier 2, or to get more information on Tier 1, such as how many extra games, how likely is it that the parents can car pool, how much more will it cost, how it will interfere with family vacation plans, and what impact it will have on the other children in the family.

If one or both parents continue to usurp, that is, make unilateral decisions, one thing the parents can do is keep a log of those situations. If a pattern becomes clear and apparent, it may be easier for the parents to recognize the pattern. Or if it becomes obvious that the parents cannot solve the problem, they may agree to see a mediator. On the other hand, both parents may have to clearly see that the consequence of not being able to agree are costly enough, that something has to be done about it. Conversely, although one parent may not be able to talk to his or her ex-spouse about their difficulty in deciding which are mutual decisions and which are not, they may be able to find someone else, such as a grandparent who can talk to their ex-spouse and work out an agreement. Lastly, if one parent continues to feel disenfranchised enough, that parent may have to make some unilateral decisions to raise the tensions to a high enough degree, so that the other parent decides that they have to do something about it.

Overlooking inclusiveness is one of the most common mistakes that ex-spouses make, and it can be a costly one because it can pervade every aspect of the negotiation process in addition to negatively impacting future negotiations. One of the best techniques to avoid this mistake is to make a list and/or a set of guidelines for what are shared decisions, which are individual decisions, and procedures and/or criteria for deciding when there is a difference of opinions.

When it comes to the children having input into the decision-making process, it always depends in part on the maturity level of the children. However, there is a rule of thumb that can prove to be very helpful. The rule of thumb states that the level of responsibility that children should have is equal to their age minus 11 times 10.

Therefore for children 11 and younger, the parents have almost full responsibility for their children. At age 12, the formula would suggest that 12 - 11 = 1 times 10, so the children are approximately 10 percent responsible. At age 17 we have 17- 11= 6 times 10, so the children are 60 percent responsible and so on until age 21, the child, now a young adult, is 100 percent responsible for his or her actions and the consequences arising from them. Remember, this is a guideline, but the guideline and any modification thereof can help separating and divorcing parents come to more mutually beneficial agreements.

It is also a good idea to look for ways to include your children in the decision-making process as long as it is appropriate to their level of maturity. For example, if the children are part of the decision-making process regarding who does what chores when, they will be more likely to be committed and hence carry out the task at hand. For those items that no one wants to do, like taking out the garbage, one fun option is to put all of the orphan chores on slips of paper and place them into a hat, and randomly draw for chores. This way everyone has an equal chance of doing those chores over time and it adds an element of fun to what could otherwise be an unpleasant negotiation for everyone involved.

In summary, master negotiators always ask themselves how much information should be shared, when it should be shared, and have well-defined boundaries on which are shared decisions and which are individual decisions. They then work to be as clear as possible about which decisions are more the ex-husband's, which decisions are more the ex-wife's, which decisions are their children's decisions or decisions where the children should have some input, and which decisions are mutual in that both parents have an equal say in making them.

No matter how clearly they work out the areas of individual versus mutual decisions, there will always be gray areas where some decisions will be or appear to be usurped by one's ex-spouse. Developing a procedure that both parties agree to on how to deal with this type of decision will go a long way in setting either a cooperative or an adversarial tone to the relationship that both ex-spouses have with each other and it will affect their children either positively or negatively. If the children see their parents working cooperatively to settle disputes that occur in the gray areas, they will learn cooperative problem-solving skills and they will not be put in a situation where they feel they have to take the side of one parent over the other. On the other hand, if the children see that their parents cannot negotiate effectively it will be harder for them to learn cooperative problem solving skills and it is much more likely that they will be put in a situation where they feel they have to take sides. This is important because how to determine what is fair and deal with what is fair is one of the most important lessons we can teach our children.

Therefore, you may want to follow the models that successful ex-spouses use regarding decision-making and develop procedures to deal with gray areas.

7. Seven Tools for Overly Cooperative Ex-Spouses

Since many of us tend to be too cooperative or too aggressive, or both, in our negotiations with our ex-spouses, this section and the next examine tools to help us not be overly cooperative or overly aggressive.

This is based on Richard G. Shell's *Bargaining for advantage: Negotiation strategies for reasonable people* (Penguin Books, 1999).

Exercise 8
Inclusiveness

1. How are we, both as ex-spouses and as our children's parents, going to consciously divide decision making authority so everyone is clear and in agreement as to which are mutual decisions and which are more the ex-wife's and ex-husband's decisions by agreement?

   Ex-Husband Decides:

   _____

   _____

   Ex-Wife Decides:

   _____

   _____

   Both Decide:

   _____

   _____

2. What types of decisions should the children be involved in?

   _____

   _____

3. What procedure(s) do we need to develop so we can resolve as effectively and constructively as possible those decisions that are or appear to be in gray areas, and/or appear to be usurped by one ex-spouse or the other?

   _____

   _____

7.1 Develop higher expectations

Research on negotiations state that we are likely to get what we expect. Overly cooperative negotiators are more likely to expect too little and subsequently receive too little. Therefore, they end up giving more than they receive and becoming resentful. They are better at creating value than claiming it. This can be even more difficult if you have a history of giving in to your ex-spouse because it has already set up the expectation that he or she will get more than he or she gives. If you have a core value of being nice and accommodating, that core value can and will be used against you.

One of the best ways to change your behavior is to set small, do-able, incremental goals such as being five percent more assertive. To put this goal into practice, you want to select three areas where you will be five percent more assertive and your goal is to be successful in only one of them. Once you have achieved success in that one area, and that success has stood the test of time, then and only then is it time to work on another goal.

Another way to change your behavior is to keep track, on a scale of 1 to 10, of how well you create value and how well you claim value. Creating value means that you expand the pie by brainstorming creative, win-win solutions. Claiming value measures how much of the pie you have after the negotiation. In general, cooperative negotiators place more value on creating value while aggressive negotiators place more value on claiming value. Master negotiators, on the other hand, do an astonishing job at both creating and claiming value. If you keep track of how well you create and claim value over time, you will be more likely to see that one of the two strategies need to be strengthened, and for the overly cooperative negotiator that means that they must do an equally good job of claiming value as they do of creating value, while the overly aggressive negotiation may need to work on creating more value, including the value of goodwill. One additional hint: rate yourself on creating and claiming value while you are in the process of negotiating because there is still time to affect the outcome.

7.2 Develop your Best Alternative To a Negotiated Agreement (BATNA)

Your Best Alternative To a Negotiated Agreement (BATNA) is your walk-away position; what you will do if the negotiation fails. One good way to develop a BATNA is to think of the worst-case scenario. For example, if you and your ex-spouse cannot agree on child visitation, public or private school, attendance at church, etc., how will you resolve the situation? In this case your BATNA could be going to court. However, it can't be your Best Alternative if you have not explored several alternatives. For example, in the example about child visitation, you and your ex-spouse could see a mediator to help you resolve your differences, and if you absolutely cannot agree on child visitation, you could ask your lawyers to work out an agreement, and if that doesn't work; you could go to family court.

Likewise, you need to look at your WATNA. If a BATNA is the Best Alternative To a Negotiated Agreement, a WATNA is your Worst Alternative To a Negotiated Agreement. If you cannot agree on child visitation and you keep the matter before the courts for years, to the point where both parties have exhausted their respective life savings, we have a good example of a WATNA. Another good example of a WATNA is a 14-year-old boy who lost 11 pounds in a hunger strike to end the custody battle between his parents.

7.3 Delegate the negotiation to someone who will be more assertive

If you feel you are overly cooperative you can delegate your negotiations to someone else, such as your lawyer, who will be more assertive than you are. Or, instead of giving in to demands, say you need some time to think about it. This will be received much more favorably if it is only used periodically. You can also use a buddy system. If your ex-spouse has a habit of bullying you and/or you have a habit of giving in, tell him or her that you need to consider what he or she has said. You then negotiate with a friend on what you will and/or will not give in to. This will help stop your automatic response to give in.

Ask for more than one alternative and/or put alternatives on the table. You can also ask creative friends, relatives, or colleagues for options to enrich the debate.

7.4 Bargain on behalf of someone or something else, not yourself

Since we tend to bargain less robustly for ourselves, pretend that you are bargaining for a friend, favorite relative, or on behalf of your children. Alternatively, find a principle that you believe in passionately, like fairness, equal rights, or a child's right to have a good relationship with both of his or her parents. Then, negotiate on behalf of that principle. Write the principle down and place it where you will see it at the start of the negotiation and all through the negotiation. That way you can start living that principle.

7.5 Create an audience

Sometimes your counterpart will negotiate much more reasonably if he or she thinks there is an audience or potential audience who would react negatively if he or she negotiated in a manner that was less than fair. As an example, Peggy states that:

> My ex-husband was being unreasonable about the scheduling of the children. As long as it was private he would be unreasonable. However, when I wrote a letter to my lawyer and he forwarded it to his lawyer, I found out that although my ex-husband didn't mind being unreasonable in front of me, he did not want to be unreasonable in front of his lawyer. After several attempts of negotiating through our lawyers, we were then able to negotiate more successfully without them. By using an audience, in this case, my ex-husband's lawyer, my ex-husband started taking me and my requests more seriously.

Remember to use consequences instead of threats. No one likes to feel threatened. Talk about your willingness and openness to use other means, and state your BATNA as an alternative to reaching an agreement by other means.

7.6 Say, "I would like you to give a little more here, because ... "

An example of "I would like you to give a little more here, because ... " would be when our 15-year-old son was a counselor in training at a summer camp and as such he was away from home for four weeks. It just so happened that my ex-wife's two-week holidays started the day he got back, and then I had the children for two weeks after that. I felt that six weeks would be a long time to go without having any contact with my son. I asked her if I could have some time with the children, maybe to take them out to dinner, during her two weeks as long as it didn't interfere with her plans.

In exchange, I offered some time when I had the children for two weeks. I thought that this might be particularly appealing, because it was during my two weeks that our son would start high school and our daughter would start junior high school. The result was a win/win/win. It was a win for both parents and for the children.

7.7 Insist on commitments, not just agreements

When is an agreement not an agreement? When it isn't in writing. Therefore when appropriate, put it in writing. For example, email has the potential to improve communications between the parties and both parties then have a written record of what their agreement or agreements were.

If there is a misunderstanding, the parties will have an early warning that the agreement wasn't as clear as both parties intended. Also, the problem will be much easier to solve when you both have some lead time, rather than waiting until you are in the middle of a crisis, based on the fact that both parties had made different assumptions.

You may remember from a previous case that William travels extensively for work, and he and his ex-spouse, Martha, had an agreement that he would be able to make the time up with his children, or at least make most of it up at a later date. However, when it came time for William to make the time up, Martha could never find a good time. When he suggested possible alternative dates, she always had a convenient excuse as to why those particular times were inconvenient. He then tried giving her a list of his travel dates a half-year in advance. Then, every time he asked what Martha thought, she said, "I didn't have a chance to look at it," or "I am still thinking about it."

Finally in desperation, William sent her a copy of the schedule and filled in the weeks he thought would work best for each of them to have the children and asked for her comments, suggestions, changes, etc. Several days later, he received a slightly modified version. In retrospect, sending his ex-wife a concrete proposal and asking for her input made a great deal of difference.

8. Seven Tools for Overly Competitive Ex-Spouses

If you are basically a competitive but still reasonable person, you need more than anything to become more aware of other people and their legitimate needs. How can you do this? It is sometimes the hardest thing in the world to overcome your inherent suspicion of others' motives. And it is difficult to resist temptation when you are dealing with a cooperative person who is naively handing things to you .

8.1 Think win-win, not win-lose

Remember that this particular negotiation is just one of a series of negotiations, and you don't want to win the battle but lose the war. Remember that your ex-spouse is still your children's mother or father. Research has shown that there is a strong correlation between the parents' self-esteem and the self-esteem of the children.

If you are a very competitive person, you will feel the need to retaliate; by nature you may be better at conflict escalation than conflict de-escalation. Therefore, you will want to train yourself in conflict de-escalation, and help the other party save face. Also, there will probably be an important favor that you will want to ask your ex-spouse for in the future. How you negotiate today will affect negotiations in the future. How you behave today will have a direct influence on how willing or unwilling your ex-spouse will be in granting a favor in the future.

8.2 Ask more questions than you think you should

You can't change someone's mind if you don't know where his or her mind is. Ask high-yield questions and use paraphrasing to make sure that you absolutely understand the other person's interests. You should be able to summarize the other person's needs more clearly, comprehensively, strongly, and powerfully than he or she can. In other words, you have to be able to articulate the other person's case at least as clearly and strongly as your own case.

8.3 Rely on standards/objective criteria

Standards are objective criteria that can help the parties reach an agreement. Standards can go from the simple to the complex.

An example would be a couple who have agreed on joint custody and joint primary residences. In other words, the children will spend 50 percent of their time at one household and 50 percent at the other household. Let's assume that the formula (50/50) works well in principle. However, each person feels that each former spouse disagrees that he or she is getting their fair share of time with the children. By actually tracking the amount of time that each parent spends with the children, the couple can then do a better job of negotiating on the merits of his or her case, and not on their ability to out debate their counterpart.

8.4 Become, find, or hire a relationship manager

There are three aspects of negotiation: the substantive outcome, the relationship outcome, and the process that will be used in the negotiation. It is natural for competitive negotiators to place most if not all of their focus on the substantive outcome. However, the substantive outcome is only one aspect of the negotiation process. You must overcome this natural tendency to focus on the substantive outcome and pay as much attention to the relationship outcome of the negotiation and the process by which the negotiation takes place.

If both parties are so focused on winning their negotiations, to the point that no one is managing the relationship variables or helping to develop the best negotiating process possible, consider hiring a relationship manager. An example of this would be when a couple hires a mediator to help manage the relationship and be a guardian of the process. Hiring a relationship manager can also be taken figuratively, such as when you ask a relative or mutual friend to play the role of mediator. There are pros and cons of hiring a mediator and pros and cons of asking a relative or friend to mediate. Using a mediator will be further explored in Chapter 9.

8.5 Be reliable

By keeping your word you have set a standard of conduct. You can then expect that your ex-spouse will be more likely to keep his or her word. This will be better for both of you and for your children. For example, if you are consistently late in bringing the children back or in picking them up, this will create problems. If your ex-spouse has the children ready and all of their belongings packed, and you keep your ex-spouse waiting because the kids are never ready, this will impact negatively on the relationship and on future negotiations.

Agreements are what make relationships work. Therefore, it is in everyone's best interests to make workable agreements, and then make those agreements work. In fact, it is probably more important that you keep your word as ex-spouses than it was when you were happily married; when you were happily married there was some extra goodwill in the bank.

8.6 Don't haggle when you can negotiate

Richard Shell (*Bargaining for Advantage*, Penguin Books, 1999) states that overly competitive negotiators are, " ... tempted to haggle over every issue and try to win each one." However, negotiations are about trade-offs. If you make sure that all of the trade-offs favor you over your ex-spouse, one of two things will happen. One, he or she will eventually become fed up and stubborn on all issues to protect himself or herself from being taken advantage of, or, two, he or she will refuse to negotiate directly thereby forcing all negotiations to go through a third party such as a lawyer. This can be expensive both economically and emotionally for both ex-spouses.

8.7 Always acknowledge the other party and protect his or her self-esteem

"People are proud. They like to hear you say they have some leverage, even when they do not. Don't gloat when you are the more powerful party. Treat people on the other side with appropriate respect. This does not cost much, and they will appreciate it. Someday they will have the leverage, and they will remember you more kindly." (*Bargaining for Advantage*, Penguin Books, 1999.) Power is a much more fluid commodity than most people realize. The shadow of the future tells us that we may be the one who wants a favor in the future. Any type of co-parenting means that there are an almost infinite number of negotiations. Sooner or later, you will want to ask your ex-spouse for a big favor, and the odds are that it will be sooner rather than later.

Develop a repository of goodwill in the relationship bank. If you are badly overdrawn, the chances of you getting your request granted diminishes exponentially. One of the best ways to make deposits into the relationship bank is to acknowledge the other party. This may be a sore issue, because lack of acknowledgement in some fundamental way could have contributed to the marital breakdown in the first place.

Just like parents are taught in parenting class, "Catch your children being good," acknowledge what your ex-spouse does well, even if he or she does not acknowledge back. This can be extremely difficult to do; however, it is important. You have to ask yourself if you want your children to have a positive role model when it comes to acknowledging people in general and people of the opposite sex in particular. Keep track of the number of negatives to positives. A simple way to do that is by keeping 10 pennies in your left pocket and 10 dimes in your right pocket. Then, every time you say something positive to or about your ex-spouse, move one penny from your left pocket to your right pocket. Every time, you say something about your ex-spouse that is negative or unpleasant, move a dime from your right pocket to your left pocket.

The results may surprise you. You may be more or less positive toward your ex-spouse than you thought you were. You may find the ratio of positive to negative statements is more skewed in the negative direction than you thought. You may find that you are just as negative to your ex-spouse as he or she is to you.

You can also do this with your children. You may find that you are more positive toward one child and more negative toward another child when you thought you treated them equally.

6

Help Your Children Enhance their Self-Esteem

Research has shown over and over that children in divided families fare better when they have two parents to enrich their lives ...

— Dr. A. Jayne Major, author of
Creating a Successful Parenting Plan: A Step- By-Step Guide for the Care of Children of Divided Families
(Breakthrough Parenting, Inc., 2002).

Parenting can be one of life's most difficult and challenging but also most rewarding experiences. Parenting after a divorce or separation can be more difficult still. First, many social resources may not be available to you. Second, if there are any areas of difficulty between the parents and/or their parenting style, it is much easier for the children to play one parent off against the other. Third, one or both parents may feel guilty that their children come from a broken family, and subsequently overindulge their children which will create future problems for some, if not all of the parties involved. Fourth, some ex-spouses use their children as bargaining chips against each other. Therefore, the purpose of this chapter is to provide you with sound advice on how to deal with each other and your children, and how to turn problems or potential problems into parenting opportunities.

1. From Guilt Mongering to Opportunity Finding

Erma Bombeck said that guilt is the gift that parents can give their children that keeps on giving. Therefore, if you are prone to guilt, in even the slightest way, going through a divorce and/or separation can be very traumatic. Society's prevailing attitude is negative, suggesting that your children now come from a broken home, and this only intensifies the guilt.

I had the wonderful opportunity of being able to teach in the Arctic where I met many Inuit. One of the most remarkable cultural differences was that if a couple or a single mother were unable to or chose not to raise a child, that child was readily adopted by another family in the community — no questions and no stigma were attached whatsoever. There is no question that children, coming from a home where there was a divorce or separation, will have to make adjustments, but one of the questions we have to frequently ask is, "Is the glass half empty or half full?" The best advice is to actively turn your concerns into opportunities without overcompensating by turning yourself and/or your ex-spouse into a "Disney Mom or Dad." One of the things that any stigmatized group must do is not engage in self-stigmatization. A divorcing or separating family must make sure that they do not stigmatize themselves as a broken family. The term "broken family" implies that it needs to be fixed because something is terribly wrong. Rather, it is an opportunity to build two new and different lives and/or families. For example, although your children may not be able to see their parents cooperating under one roof, they can see their parents cooperating under two roofs. If you lose one tradition, you can create new ones. If you have less time with your children in terms of quantity, you can increase the amount of quality time you have with your children.

2. Focus on What You Can Do for Your Children, Not on What You Can't Do

After they separated, Brian and Stephanie bought homes on the same cul-de-sac. Although they could not physically see each other's homes, it was very easy for the children to visit both parents and the parents could easily change nights if necessary. However, the best thing that Brian and Stephanie did was they decided to have dinner together with their two children once a week and the dinner alternates between their two homes. Although the initial reason for having their weekly dinner was that it would be a time when everyone could catch up on what happened during the past week and inform each other of the activities that would take place during the upcoming week. Stephanie and Brian describe additional benefits of their weekly dinner as follows.

> **Stephanie said:** It's all about the children and how we communicate. I feel that we are able to show our children that even though their parents don't live together, they can still be respectful, considerate, friendly, and even loving. We came together because we loved one another and our children are a product of that love.
>
> Because we love our children so much, we have committed to moving beyond the characteristics that didn't work and focus on the positive characteristics that do. In other words, we have learned to love each other, warts and all.
>
> I am so grateful that my partner is such a good father and I am very grateful that we can respect each other and support each other as parents and that our children can see it.
>
> **Brian said:** The Sunday dinner is an extension of what we did when we were married. When we were married we used the Sunday dinner as an exchange of information and ideas. We used that dinner as a lead-in to understand what was going on with the children and each other when we were married. I come from a big family where there were seven children, and the Sunday family dinner is a part of my personal history. My six siblings and I are as tight now as we were 20 years ago. The kitchen table was key to our being a family.
>
> When we separated, I wanted to show my children that even though the marriage did not continue, the family does. Our youngest child is four years old and I wanted him to have an idea of what a family is, I didn't want him to grow up not knowing what it was like to be a part of a family. We were able to keep this family tradition. So every Sunday, when we have our family dinner, we catch up, exchange schedules and ideas. We help each other cook and put the kids to bed together. Some traditions are worth keeping and this is one that we have chosen to keep.

Although you can't have some of the old traditions, at least not in the old way, you can have new traditions.

Opportunity Finding

List all of the creative opportunities you can find or use to improve the quality of the time you spend with your children and/or brainstorm opportunities with your children.

2.1 Write a family mission statement

Going through a separation and divorce is a major life transition. Feelings of guilt and self-recriminations are likely to be particularly strong at first. Sadness and not being able to kiss my children goodnight or see them wake up in the morning was extremely difficult, however, after what seemed like a very long time I realized that this was not just a time of endings, but also a time of new beginnings with the net result that I have a stronger relationship with my children now that I am divorced than I ever did when I was married, although it was impossible to have perspective at the time I was going through my separation.

One of the things that you can do, and this was especially helpful for me in the early stages of my separation, is to write a mission statement for yourself and your children. For your purposes, it doesn't matter if you call it a mission statement, vision, or a stewardship agreement.

My stewardship agreement helped me to focus on what I could provide, not on what I couldn't provide. It helped me see that I still had a clear purpose and a valuable role to play. It also helped me remember my mission statement because I put a copy of it on the refrigerator door where I could see it on a daily basis. I believe that this also helped my children see more clearly what my intentions were.

Exercise 10
Mission Statement

Write a mission statement for yourself and your children. It is a good idea to date your mission statement and modify it or change it entirely as is necessary. Lastly, you may want to share your mission statement with your children and get their input and/or place your mission statement in a place where you will see it every day to reinforce that you have a plan and are committed to making your new family work.

2.2 Increase your children's self-esteem

Family counselor and self-esteem expert Vince MacDonald suggests that, "Divorcing parents can really help their children if they pay attention to the building blocks of self-esteem which includes building a sense of security, belonging, self identity, purpose and competency." What Vince says is true for divorced and non-divorced parents alike. As parents we should actively look for ways to develop and enhance our children's self-esteem.

There are all kinds of activities and organizations where children can develop and enhance their sense of self and self-esteem. Among the activities and organizations that separating and divorcing parents have praised in helping their children develop self-esteem are: any type of sport and musical activity, Boy Scouts, Girl Guides, 4-H and other specialty clubs, churches, synagogues, mosques, etc.

> Sid said that his 12-year-old daughter, Shelly, joined the debating club at her junior high school a year and a half after Sid and his wife, Heather, separated. A local lawyer, who was a former champion debater, comes each week to adjudicate, and the children take turns being debaters, time keepers, as well as being asked for their individual comments. Sid reports that he has seen his daughter both learn about and become better informed about various subjects from gun control to recycling. At one point one of the debaters from their local senior high school came to observe and coach.
>
> When he finished, he told Shelly that she and her team were as good as the average debater in his high school. That night, Shelly told a proud Sid, about the compliment that she and her team had been given. Sid said, "I could almost see her self-esteem grow before my very own eyes."

Each of these activities and organizations can help your child grow and develop skills and a sense of self. Your children can also be exposed to new, varied, and supportive role models. On the negative side, too many activities and organizations can give your child a place to hide from the pain that they may be experiencing, which in excess can be a bad thing because the child will never learn to deal with his or her problems and concerns. You as the parent must do everything to make sure that your children are exposed to good role models and help them cope with the occasional poor one.

3. Increase Positive Feedback

Vince MacDonald also suggests that we look for something every day for which you can say thank you to your children. Vince advocates writing notes to our children. For example, in addition to telling your children what they are doing well, use Post-It Notes and/or write brief comments and put them in an envelope under your children's pillows. Knowing that you have taken the time to write, and because letter-writing and the written word occur so infrequently in today's society, your written comments will stand out. One parent even printed out postcards that said, "You've Done Well" complete with space to fill in the details.

For example, one of the notes I gave Katie said: "You are an A+ conversationalist. I especially like the way you ask me how my day went, and then really listen to what I have to say." One of the notes I gave Andrew said: "You are an A+ team player on your hockey team. I love the way you play your defensive position strategically and support your goalie."

3.1 Family report cards

Over the years I have watched with interest how both of my children anticipated and took pride in their report cards. This inspired me to give each of my children a family report card. An added benefit is that each mark caused much debate and increased the amount of valuable information all of the parties were able to contribute and deal with. I knew that my children liked this idea when they each gave me my own report card. Also note, that it is interesting to compare one year's report cards with the next to help highlight any improvements, or lack thereof.

Katie's Report Card	2001	2002	2003
Responsibility at school	A+	A+	A+
Responsibility in trying new activities	A	A	A
Responsibility for chores	B	C	B-
Responsibility in soccer	A	A+	A+
Responsibility in acknowledging Dad	B	A-	A-
Andrew's Report Card			
Responsibility at school	A	A	A+
Responsibility for chores	B	B	B+
Responsibility in hockey	A	A	A

Responsibility in having meaningful conversations with Dad	C-	C+	B
Responsibility in watching out for Katie	A+	A	A
Responsibility in music	A+	A	A+

Dad's Report Card	Andrew	Katie
Responsibility at work	A	A+
Responsibility in driving Kids to activities	B	B-
Responsibility in keeping the house clean	C	C
Responsibility in cooking delicious meals	B-	C+
Responsibility in having fun	C	C+
Responsibility in planning trips & vacations	A	A

3.2 Family trophies

In their book, *1001 Ways to Reward Employees*, (Workman Publishing, 2005), Bob Nelson and Kenneth Blanchard suggest getting a new or used trophy to help acknowledge an employee for a job that has been particularly well done. Then, every week the trophy is given to another employee who has made a difference at work. Well, you can do the same thing within your family. I bought a second-hand trophy. My children liked having a trophy so much, that at one point they took it over to their mother to acknowledge her contributions in their other family.

There are many ways to build your children's self-esteem during difficult transitions, but it takes a conscious effort on your part to do so. Family trophies, Post-It Notes, and family report cards are only three.

4. Seize Opportunities for Role Expansion

Being divorced or separated allows both parents to expand their roles as parents. Before we divorced, my wife did all of the children's medical and dental appointments, and most of the parent-teacher interviews, while I did most of the lawn and car care and driving to and from sporting events. After we separated, we both had cars and lawns to take care of, so I started going to doctor's appointments and school meetings. First, it was an opportunity to spend more time with the children, which I value greatly, and second, it is very interesting and refreshing to get an entirely different perspective on my children from their teachers' points of view. I knew that our children were good students, but to see how highly they were valued as individual contributors by their teachers was truly gratifying.

Victor, one of the fathers I interviewed, reported the following changes.

> One big change is that I do more cooking now than I did when I was married. It was rather rough going at first and the children were more than critical of my culinary experiments. However, I learned how to expand my repertoire of recipes. The other thing that happened is that each child is now responsible for helping me cook and/or doing the dishes on a daily rotation. I found out that they were much less critical of food when they helped prepare it. They tended to be more complimentary because they [began to realize] how much work is involved. An added benefit is that we have had some of our best conversations while cooking and/or cleaning up together.

5. Use Behavioral Analysis

You can use behavioral analysis to help determine if something is really an issue or a pet peeve. Behavioral analysis means that we actually count the number of times a specific behavior occurs or does not occur. We can then use these systematic observations to determine if there is really a problem, if it is a pet peeve to which we are overreacting, or some combination of both.

For example, my daughter started saying no to what seemed to be my every request. So I started counting the number of times she said yes versus the number of times that she said no. She was up to 11 nos and 1 yes when the message started to sink in. The thing that happened next was that the children started making a great number of unreasonable requests to improve the yes-to-no ratio. For example they both asked me to buy them a Porsche. However, at least this one time, I was one step ahead of them. I never technically said no. They never technically said what size Porsche they wanted. So I stopped into a local Toys-R-Us store and purchased two $5 Porsches and made the presentation at a family dinner. Now, I was sure that this was only round one in the yes/no ratio game and I was looking forward to their comeback!

The point is that behavioral analysis helps us to see what is really going on by actually seeing how many times different events occur or do not occur. For example, Jill was having difficulty getting her two children to walk Julia, the family dog. First, both children agreed that they wanted to keep the dog and that walking the dog two times a day for 45 minutes was reasonable. The children were asked to keep track on the calendar every time they walked the dog and the calendar would show if their behavior was equal to their promise. Keeping track of walking on the calendar did result in a 100 percent improvement.

6. Maintain Family Traditions and Develop New Ones

In his pioneering research on children from alcoholic families, Dr. Steve Wolin, asked a very interesting question in his keynote address entitled, "Discovering Resiliency: Children at Risk," at the annual meeting of the American Association of Marriage and Family Therapy in Dallas, Texas, in 1991. Why were some of the children from families of alcoholics resilient while others were not?

One of the results from this research that is most pertinent for divorcing or separating parents who are raising children has to do with traditions. The children from alcoholic families who kept their traditions intact, in spite of being alcoholic — such as Thanksgiving, Christmas, birthdays, summer holidays, and family vacations — were much more resilient than the children from alcoholic families where the traditions were not kept intact. Wolin goes on to state that, "Rituals are the times that weave the web of group and family identity." These family rituals and traditions help people develop pride in themselves and in their families. Therefore, we want to keep as many rituals and traditions as possible and support our ex-spouses in doing the same.

For example, when Michele and Al were married, they used to spend alternate New Years' with the children and with adult friends. When they separated, they made sure that they could keep this tradition from their old family to their new families. One of the traditions that I started years ago was a Summer Solstice Party to celebrate the longest day of the year (or the closest Saturday to it) with friends, and other families and their children. I remember one year feeling particularly tired and I mentioned that we might not have the Summer Solstice Party that year. It was only after my children kicked up such a fuss and said that they were willing to help with all of the preparations that I realized how important this tradition had become to them.

I found Wolin's findings so interesting and the fact that the Christmas holidays are such an emotional time for many people, that I made it a point to ask the people I interviewed for this book how they spent their holidays. For example, when I asked Rosie, who shared a flat with her ex-spouse, how they celebrated the holidays, she replied:

> We partly celebrate Christmas as a nuclear family and partly as two separate families. For example, we always have a meal together either Christmas Eve or Christmas Day, and my ex-husband's current girlfriend usually joins us for that meal. The girls open their presents upstairs with their father first thing Christmas morning and then everyone comes downstairs and they open their presents at my house.

Likewise, I asked another divorced couple, Heather and Marty, about how they handled the holidays. Heather said:

> All of our sons are married and we have 3 grandchildren. We all go to Marty's house for Thanksgiving. They all come to my house on Christmas Eve and we all have Christmas dinner at one of our son's houses. I am very thankful for this, because we are still very much a family even though Marty and I have been separated for 12 years now.

6.1 Surprise trips and outings

Every once in a while I take my children on surprise trips and outings. Sometimes we go together and often I take them separately. For example, several years ago, I planned a surprise for my daughter Katie. Katie was 100 percent sure that we were going to Ottawa but we were actually going to Boston. Part of the fun of the trip was that Katie didn't know from one minute to the next what we were going to do. While we were having a great dinner at a Vietnamese restaurant, I told Katie that the next day we would go to Harvard to get Andrew a souvenir if the weather was good, or if it were raining cats and dogs, we would go to the science museum. I was surprised when Katie asked me if the expression "raining cats and dogs" was a clue. I said, "What do you mean?" and Katie asked me if we came to Boston to get a puppy. Actually, the reason for the trip was that I had been able to get tickets for Riverdance.

The most important part of these surprise trips and outings is that they allow us to really connect away from the rigors of daily life.

Exercise 11
Surprise Outings

Are there some surprise outings you could plan for each of your children individually or together? The outing doesn't need to cost a great deal of money. Arranging a scavenger hunt through your city or town could be just as exciting as a major trip. The important thing to remember is how much all of us like being surprised.

6.2 Capture family history

One of the traditions that I have continued is to write a yearly Christmas letter. Although the original purpose of the letter was to stay in contact with friends and relatives, I noticed that the letter also served as a vehicle for capturing some of our family history. I now continue this tradition, not only to stay in contact with friends and relatives, but more importantly to keep a record of our accomplishments individually and as a family. I now have a collection of these letters dating back to 1993, and when the children turn 21, I will give them each a specially bound book that has our history to date with lots of room for future installments.

Exercise 12
Family Traditions

Which family traditions do you want to make sure you keep intact?

Are there any family traditions you want to start in your new family?

7. Keep Extended Families Intact

Some of the most tragic stories that are associated with divorce and separation are when one of the parents kidnaps his or her own children or when parental wars turn into family wars, or the children lose contact with their grandparents and other relatives. However, some of the people I interviewed who impressed me the most were ex-spouses, who in spite of their individual differences, were able to keep their extended families intact. Two of those stories follow.

Warren is twice divorced. He has a daughter, Emily, from his first marriage with June. When they were married, June had another daughter, Elizabeth, from her first marriage, which made Warren Elizabeth's stepfather. Warren and Elizabeth had and still have a very close relationship. This also made Emily and Elizabeth half-sisters. Both Warren and June have since remarried, and June and her new husband, Dick, also had a daughter, Michele. This makes Emily, Elizabeth, and Michele stepsisters.

Warren then married Evelyn and they had a son, Zachary. When Warren and Evelyn divorced, Evelyn married Randy and they also had a son, Ryan. So that makes Emily and Zachary half-siblings and Zachary and Ryan half-brothers. When I interviewed Warren, he said:

> Scheduling can be a nightmare as is keeping track of everyone's relationship to everyone else. In fact, when I meet people and they ask me if I have children, I never know how to answer because it can take me fifteen minutes to get all of the relationships straight, and by that time the other person is totally confused. It is also true that at any given time, at least one of the former spouses isn't getting along with one of the other former spouses, and that is hard to keep track of as well.
>
> What is working well is that several times a year, parts of our extended network, and sometimes the whole network, gets together for the sake of the children who all like each other most of the time. And frankly, when we do get together and I watch the children interact, it reminds me of some of my fondest childhood memories when my extended family got together and I could play with various cousins.

During the process of writing this book, I asked everyone I knew if they knew anyone who was divorced and who had a positive story about the experience. As a result, one of the most delightful interviews I had was with an 82-year-old grandmother named Florence. Florence is a widow who had been married for over 56 years to Fred before he passed away 8 years ago. In describing her own marriage, she said, "We had our ups and downs just like any couple, but we complemented each other in the important parts." Florence and Fred had three children: Lisa, Samantha, and Darrell. All three of her children had married and had children themselves. Both Lisa and Darrell are also divorced. At the present time Lisa has remarried, while Darrell had remarried, divorced, and was now living common-law. Every summer, Florence invites everyone to her home, and I mean everyone — her son, her daughters, their ex-spouses, their ex-spouse's current spouses or boyfriends or girlfriends, and all of the children. Florence reports that:

My friends of my generation thought I was crazy to invite everyone home, but I liked every last one of them and they liked me. As far as I am concerned, once you are part of my family, you are always part of my family, and you are always welcome at my house. Also, I think you are giving me way too much credit. They are all good and loving people and they all had children and some very good years together. They didn't separate because there were any infidelities; they separated because they became incompatible.

I feel blessed that they each have had a good divorce but I wept when they told me. You can be good friends without being good lovers as opposed to my generation when almost everyone stuck together no matter what. So I try to be open minded and it usually pays off. All they needed was an opportunity to see that they still liked each other. So when I invited everyone for the Millennium Party, they all came. For my part, I'm interested in life and I am interested in people and that keeps me young.

After talking to Florence, I could understand why this works. Florence genuinely likes people and it was easy to see why people liked Florence. It took me a little while to get an appointment to talk to her because she was so busy with her family, friends, and decorating the church basement for an upcoming function. The best single way to describe Florence is that she exudes zest. She is a great example of maintaining family traditions and contact, even after divorce.

What do these stories tell us? First, there is a huge diversity of types of relationships that former spouses can have, and some of these relationships are worth keeping even if conventional wisdom is that they can't be or shouldn't be kept intact.

Exercise 13
Relationships

Are there any relationships that you would like to maintain or reinstate? If so, please list those relationships in the space below and outline your plan to do so.

Who might stand in your way of maintaining or reinstating these relationships? How will you deal with the resistance?

8. Sometimes It's Not the Big Issues but the Overabundance of Small Ones

It is absolutely true that stress can be caused by major events, but it is also absolutely true that an overabundance of small ones can be equally and sometimes even more difficult. In this section we will look at how several families have dealt with the smaller issues one at a time.

Louise said that in the five years since she and her ex-husband Bud had separated and divorced, they had successfully resolved all of the major issues regarding division of property and making arrangements for a flexible but fair parenting agreement that included who had the children when. And for the most part, it felt to her that they shared the parenting responsibilities equitably. However, it was the overabundance of small things that continued to cause stress. For example, Louise gave their children Robbie, aged 13, and Christine, aged 10, new winter gloves for Christmas. On Boxing Day, both children were with their Dad and Christine brought her new gloves and matching headband over to her Dad's and duly put them away. Robbie decided to help Dad out by shoveling the sidewalk after the big Christmas Day snowstorm. The only problem was that he used Christine's new gloves which were then, according to Christine, stretched out of shape and ruined. Bud then had a serious talk with Robbie about using other people's things without permission. That evening, Louise, Bud, Robbie, and Christine sat down to a family meeting about the gloves and other related issues. Robbie said that the gloves were the same color as his and he thought he was using his own. Louise said that maybe Robbie should buy Christine a new set of gloves.

Bud said that maybe Robbie should be told the consequences before they were put into effect, or maybe he should have to pay half for a new pair of gloves. In the end, Louise countered that she would wash them and put them in the dryer and see if she could return them to their original condition. If not, Robbie agreed to pay for half the price of a new pair. Bud promised to buy some gloves for his house as well as place a divider in the glove drawer so it would be easier to distinguish between Robbie's and Christine's gloves. This would also make it easier for Robbie to see if he had gloves at both houses. Lastly, everyone agreed that the children should have multiple gloves of the same kind which would help if one was lost, and that both Robbie and Christine should have gloves of different colors.

What did Louise and Bud do right? First they had a family meeting because it was a family issue and it could only really be completely resolved at the family level. Second, they looked at how they could best solve the problem in the future rather than engage in fault finding in the past. Third, they placed multiple options on the table and agreed to a multi-pronged approach that gave responsibility to each family member for helping to solve the problem.

> At the same family meeting, they discussed that Louise had planned to visit her parents who lived about an hour away. This was a perfect opportunity for Robbie to go snowboarding as the ski hill was on the way to his grandparent's house. Robbie then thought it would be a great opportunity for his buddies to go boarding with him so they decided to all spend the night together before the first snowboarding adventure of the year. This meant that the children would stay at Louise's even though it was Bud's night to have the children. However, there was enough flexibility between the parents so they just swapped nights and it seemed that everything was settled.

> That is, it was settled until Christine realized that she and Robbie were not being treated equally because Robbie got to go snowboarding and she did not. Both parents explained to Christine that she was too young to go snowboarding without adult supervision. And although Christine's concerns were acknowledged, and this did a lot to make them go away, she still felt hard done by, at least until Bud promised to take her snowboarding at some point during the holiday.

When I interviewed Doug, he told me that he and his ex-wife Martha had dealt with all of the major issues regarding their separation and divorce. However, the issue that Doug told me about was that he was left feeling like the provider, cook, chauffeur,and felt miffed that there was little time when he and his son Mathew, and daughter Belinda did anything together. Doug says that both his children were good students; good athletes, and both have great friends. However, between being with their friends, talking to their friends on the phone (Doug said that he has long since assumed that the calls were not for him), and the Internet, it was hard to get the children to commit to family time. Doug further stated that, although he was able to spend quality time alone with each child, he very much wanted to have more quality time when the three of them could spend time together. The one area where they were successful was that they watched Malcolm in the Middle together on television on Sunday nights.

Doug decided to start small and gradually increase. Doug declared that there would be one time each month when the three of them would engage in dedicated family time. They would each take a turn picking the activity. Although there was a major rebellion at first, Doug stood his ground and said that this was non-negotiable. It also helped that Doug explained what he was doing using an analogy.

He took a mayonnaise jar and said that the jar represented a bank. He put in $10 and said that each dollar represented goodwill. He then said that when Mathew wanted to be driven to his basketball practice, it represented a $1 withdrawal of goodwill; likewise when Belinda wanted to be picked up after the movie with her friends. Doug continued to take out dollars for various things he did for the children. He then put in $2 to represent the children and took out some more until the bank was empty.

He then emphasized to the children that if they wanted to continue to take out, they needed to put more in. Somewhat reluctantly, the children eventually got the message.

Now, several nights per month, they play games together and Doug reports that they feel more like a family, which is important to him and he does things both for and with the children more freely.

Sometimes changes have to be imposed rather than negotiated. The bank analogy helped the children understand Doug's request and the balance between the teenagers need for autonomy and Doug's need for the family as a whole to get its fair share of time is in much better balance.

Remember the old saying, "How do you eat an elephant? One bite at a time." For some families, the key to success is to resolve one issue at a time and get closure on that issue before going on to the next. In other cases if a family tries to resolve one issue at a time, it won't work because the issues are too interrelated. In cases like these, nothing can get resolved or accomplished unless all of the issues are put on the table and resolved at the same time.

7
Model Good Conflict Resolution Strategies

Family therapist Virginia Satir said, "You cannot not communicate." Likewise, communication expert Marshall McLuhan stated, "The medium is the message." The bottom line is that you are communicating, often loud and clear — only you have chosen to communicate non-verbally instead than verbally. In other words, how people communicate is as important if not more important than what they communicate, because they are teaching their children how to communicate. Even by not communicating, you are communicating that you don't want to speak at the present time, or that you are angry, or that you wish to punish the other party by not communicating.

For example, Rob's ex-wife, Roxanne, makes it abundantly clear that she does not like him, even without saying a word. When Rob comes to the house to pick up their children, Robbie and Karen, Roxanne, almost always greets Rob with a long, cold, hostile glare. Also Roxanne's house does not have a porch and Rob almost always has to stay on the front steps, where there is no covering even when it is raining.

Consider the law of unintended consequences. The law of unintended consequences states that sometimes the things that we do have unintended consequences and those unintended consequences can be good or bad. Taking these three principles into consideration: 1) you cannot not communicate, 2) the medium is the message, and 3) the law of unintended consequences, divorcing and separating couples must pay very close attention to the types of conflict resolution strategies they use and to the types of conflict resolution strategies they are teaching their children.

For example, as I was writing this chapter, I received a telephone call from my 15-year-old son Andrew. It was 8:30 Sunday morning and both children were at their mother's house because her week was ending and my week was to start at 4:00 p.m. that afternoon. I was surprised to hear my son's cheerful voice that early in the morning, until he said that he and some buddies were going to go snowboarding and his mother had agreed to pick them up after skiing so he would probably be late coming to my house. He then asked, "Is that a problem?"

I said, "Being late isn't a problem; however, [getting to] your hockey tournament might be." Andrew and his team had been in the annual Christmas tournament. His team won a tough game the night before and had secured a place in tonight's championship game. They had played the other championship team once already in the tournament so it was sure to be a closely fought game. The other piece of information you need to have to understand this situation is that Andrew had gone snowboarding on Friday before the game and certainly did not play as well as he usually did and the most likely cause was that he was tired from snowboarding. I asked Andrew's mother to get on the other phone so both parents could discuss the situation with Andrew. In the end, his mother and I agreed that he could go snowboarding, and she would pick him and his friends up at 4:00 p.m. Since the championship game was at 9:00 p.m., this would give him a chance to rest and do some walking to get his legs into shape for the hockey game.

I felt that this was a very good outcome. Andrew saw his parents cooperating. We were able to honor his interest in going snowboarding and our interest that he keep his commitment to his hockey team. This also sets a positive precedent as to how we could and should negotiate in the future.

1. The Put-Down Parent

It is natural for one or both parents to feel angry, hurt, disappointed, and/or betrayed by the other. It is also natural to feel unloved and sometimes unlovable. It is also natural to feel competitive with an ex-partner, and it is natural for you to compete with an ex-partner for the attention and love of your children. However, for your children's sake, don't do it.

In most cases, the children are facing one of the most difficult transitions in their lives as well. They need to know that they have the love and support of both parents. That said, the darker side of human nature sometimes takes over, and one or both parents may find that they are putting down or being put down by the other. As children are more perceptive than we give them credit for, they will either experience the put-downs directly, or indirectly through overheard conversations, or more subtly still by picking up the bad vibes that one parent sends out about the other.

Five of the best techniques you can use with the put-down parent are covered in the next sections.

1.1 Name the game but let him or her save face

If your ex-spouse says something that sounds like a put-down, ask if that particular statement is a put-down. Even if it is and he or she says no, you have named the game, you have stood up for yourself, and you didn't resort to an unproductive cycle of attack/counter attack. Psychologists have demonstrated that if a behavior does not have the impact that it was intended to have, that behavior will most likely extinguish. Extinguish means that the behavior will most likely stop occurring or will occur less frequently over time, although in the short term it might actually increase. Think of someone pounding on a vending machine that does not deposit the desired object after the customer puts in his or her money. At first, the customer may pound on the machine, but eventually he or she will walk away.

1.2 Ask what the other person would have done in that particular situation

Another good technique is to ask your ex-spouse what he or she would have done in your shoes. If he or she has a better idea, you can choose to use it in the present situation or at a future date. If your ex remains silent, you have made your point.

If you really want to be scientific, keep a notepad and write down the put-down and/or the number of put-downs. Then try one of these interventions and see if the number of put downs increase or decrease over time. One of the side benefits of doing this type of analysis is that it puts you in the role of observer and most people can be more detached when they are in that particular role.

1.3 Point out what is working well

One of the best ways to stop the put-down artist in his or her tracks is to do the opposite of the expected response. Instead of sinking to his or her level with your own put-down, point out the areas where the two of you are working well together for the benefit of the children. Often the put-down artist will be at a loss for words because your reaction was so unexpected.

1.4 Ask the other person if he or she supports your child or children in having a good relationship with both parents

This technique can be particularly effective if you have a shared parenting agreement where you both acknowledge that your child or children need to have a strong relationship with both parents. Since questions tend not to be accusatory, it is a good idea to phrase your request in as neutral a language as possible.

1.5 Anticipate the put-down

One of the things that you can do is to anticipate the put-down and change your self-talk at the same time. An example of how one of the women I interviewed, Betsey, sought counseling and learned several strategies to deal with her ex-husband's put-downs follows.

> My ex-husband Bert is one of the best put-down artists around and I am tired of being his target. One of the things that makes put downs, which are a type of bullying, so difficult is that I never know when they will occur. One of the techniques I learned in counseling is how to deal with it proactively rather than reactively.
>
> My counselor asked me to think of Bert as an Olympic level put-down artist. She then suggested that when he puts me down that I rate it on a scale of one to ten for its level of creativity. For example, a level one put down would be, "You are late again. Why can't you ever be on time?" This would be a level one put-down because it is not very creative. A level five put-down was, "How thoughtful of you to forget to remind the children to call my mom on her birthday," and a level ten put-down would be remarking what a bad parent I am, or bad person in front of the children. Rating the level of creativity of the put-down helped me move into an analytic observer position rather than reacting emotionally to it.

At this point, my counselor told me I had a choice. I could either use the strategy silently or I could start assigning marks on the level of creativity orally. Both strategies tend to minimize the impact and your level of reaction to put-downs. If giving the marks orally tends to make the situation worse, do it silently to yourself. Remember, one of Eleanor Roosevelt's most famous sayings is "No one can make you feel bad without your permission." Therefore, one of the things I do is write the put-downs on a piece of paper, and then write out an appropriate response. In most cases I keep the responses to myself to avoid escalating the situation, but at certain times, I will use them to show him that I will not be bullied.

One last technique my counselor taught me is to imagine that I could actually see myself, in my mind's eye, as Teflon-coated, and actually see the put-down slipping off the surface as it crashes onto the ground far below me.

The fact that you cannot not communicate, the medium is the message, and there is a law of unintended consequences can have negative outcomes as well as positive outcomes, as is illustrated in the following example of Gary.

From the outside, we looked like the ideal family. We had two great children, a son and a daughter; a wonderful house on a lake in the country; shared many of the same hobbies and sports; and had one of the best friendship networks possible. When our relatives and friends found out that we were splitting up, it sent shock waves throughout our community. I can't tell you how many people told us that they thought we were the ideal couple and would be the last couple that any of them thought would ever split up.

What no one knew, and we were able to hide it from everyone, including our children was that we were both very unhappy. We both had an affair; the only difference was that Dawn's affair turned into a long-term love relationship. We sold the house, moved into the city. We both bought houses in the same neighborhood; luckily the lakeside property had appreciated a great deal. We both had the utmost respect for each other as parents so we never even considered any option other than shared and equal parenting. I had assumed that this meant a week on and a week off, or something similar, until Dawn, seemingly from out of the blue, said that her preferred option was a year on and a year off, with me taking the children for the first year and Dawn and her new partner having the children every second weekend and alternating Wednesday nights.

It took me a long time to agree, but the thought of not putting the children to bed at night and seeing them first thing in the morning was very traumatic and troubling for me, even though I knew that the second year would be impossibly difficult, and even though my own intuition was that this was not a good idea, I eventually gave in and said yes.

In the end, I felt taken advantage of. The real purpose of this arrangement was so that Dawn could establish her new relationship. One of the unintended consequences was that while our son and daughter went through the very difficult transition of us separating, they lived with and relied on me as their primary parent. And although the children are close to, and are loyal to their mother, they still consider me as their primary parent today, some 12 years later. And although they are now both grown and off to college, I am afraid that I didn't teach them to be as assertive as they should be, just like I wasn't as assertive as I should have been. I also feel that they felt somewhat abandoned by their mother, and I hope and pray that that won't become a problem as they enter their own long term relationships.

Here's another story from Bev.

Charles, my husband, and I have a wonderful relationship, but we had a hard time with his children accepting us. Right from the get go, I was painted as the ugly step-mother. Lucy, my husband's ex, took all of her aggression and unhappiness out on my husband Charles and myself; the biggest problem was that she did this indirectly through the children rather than directly to us. It didn't take long for us to realize that Charles was painted as the philandering husband and I was labeled as "that loose woman," even though we started dating months after the separation. Unfortunately, the children bought their mother's propaganda and treated both their father and myself with a great deal of disrespect. However, over the summer, when the children stayed with us for a month and a half solid, they got to see how happy Charles and I were, how respectfully we treated each other, and how respectfully we treated them and their relationship with their mother. Two years later, the eldest child has chosen to live with us and the youngest is considering moving in with us as well. I think they both got fed up with their mother's unhappiness, blaming everything on Charles and me rather than getting on with her own life. The children were really more perceptive than any of us gave them credit for. The unintended consequence was that in trying to poison the children's relationship with their father, Lucy actually poisoned her relationship with her children.

Another example of bad unintended consequences is the triangling parent.

2. The Triangling Parent

Triangling is the process where one party gets in the way of, obstructs, tries to prevent, and/or comes between two other people. Part of the goal of many forms of family therapy is to help the parties de-triangle and therefore relate to each other directly rather than through a third party. An example of triangling would be that every time a father tries to spend some time with his daughter, the mother intervenes and says that their daughter has homework that she has to complete.

It is worth noting that triangling can be subtle or not-so-subtle, and can happen between some family members and not others. An example of a more subtle form of triangling would be a father who discourages his son from talking with his mother. For example, when the son has an issue with his mother, the father encourages the son to talk to him about his concerns with his mother, rather than talking with his mother directly. Please note that some triangling in the form of helping the parties to communicate and/or playing the role of mediator is healthy. Overdoing it, and/or coming between two parties that should have open and free-flowing communication is not.

Here is a letter I once received.

> Dear Expert Negotiator: I have two children, a son aged 15 and a daughter aged 12. My ex-wife and I each have the children 50 percent of the time. The problem I have is that my ex-wife calls my daughter frequently and tends to talk to her for relatively long periods of time. The problem this creates of me is that I have more difficulty bonding with my daughter when she is in my house and my daughter has more difficulty settling in. What makes matters worse

is that she seems to always call just as we are getting ready to have dinner, or watch one of our favorite television shows or a movie. What should I do?

— *Feeling Intruded Upon In Iowa*

Dear FIUII: The first thing you need to do is bring this issue to your ex-spouse's attention. She may not realize how much she is calling or that you find it intrusive. After gently pointing out your concerns, your ex-spouse may change her behavior. Second, if you have a co-parenting agreement, and the co-parenting agreement states that you will both support each other in being the best parent you can be, you may be able to invoke the agreement and the behavior may subsequently change.

Third, you could ask that she not call during meal hours unless it is an emergency or special circumstance. Fourth, you could ask your ex-spouse to time her calls, and/or you can time the calls and then discuss know how much time is involved. Fifth, you can bring the problem to the attention of your daughter and gently state your concerns and ask her how she would like to handle the problem. Sixth, if the problem persists, consider mediation.

3. Double Binds

Double binds are psychological traps, where you are damned if you do and damned if you don't. One of the properties of traps is that they can trap one and often both ex-spouses, and the children as well. An all-too-common example of a double bind is "the broken promise parent."

3.1 The broken promise parent

Some of the most heartbreaking stories I have heard revolved around a parent who would make repeated promises to both an ex-spouse and the children, but seldom keep them. This can put the other parent in a double bind. If you say something negative about the other parent who breaks promises you run the risk of escalating the situation. If you don't say anything, you have to live with the hurt and pain your children feel when the other parent doesn't keep his or her word or doesn't show up. You have three main strategies to choose from: 1) Try to talk to your ex-spouse as positively as possible, 2) ask a third party to talk to your ex-spouse, and/or 3) try to inoculate your child or children against the stress and trauma of your ex-spouse's broken promises. Just as we can inoculate our children against diseases such as mumps and rubella, psychological Donald Michenbaum has proved that we can inoculate ourselves and our children against stress. For example, have something fun that you and the children can do to ease the sense of disappointment and use this as an opportunity to teach your children resiliency. If your ex-spouse has other good or great traits, acknowledge those traits to your children and where appropriate, turn the situation into a lesson where you point out the importance of keeping your word. Another problem occurs when a former spouse favors one child over another as in Tracey's story.

> My ex-husband was treating our son and daughter differently after we separated. For example, he would buy more presents and more expensive presents for our son than he would for our daughter. When I confronted him on this, he usually played "poor me." Our daughter always came to me when she saw that her brother was given more things and more opportunities than she was. I tried to make up for this, but really didn't have the money to make things even. I then asked her why she came to me and she said that she knew me better and was more comfortable talking with me. I eventually took myself out of the role of go-between and told her that she would be treated more equally if she negotiated directly with her father. I also explained that when I negotiated, it was hard for him to hear me because of our past relationship and it just got in the way.

> I kept encouraging her to go to the source. I even role-played the situation with her playing herself and me playing the role of her father so she wouldn't feel intimidated. Eventually she got up her nerve and was able to talk to her dad and the situation improved immediately.

I asked Tracey how she developed the self-control not to intervene because I could just imagine how upset I would be if anyone were to treat my two children that differently. Tracey said:

> At first I would get pissed off because it made me so mad just to have to talk to him. He would do "poor me" and I would just go bananas. Then somebody said, "Just don't listen to him," but I didn't know how I could do that until one day I put the phone down so I could hear the voice, but not the words — that way I wouldn't respond emotionally. I also learned that he had to just get through his wall of words. I already knew the message, so I didn't have to listen to the words.

Then when he would wind down, I would say something like, "I understand," and then go on to make my point in a very reasonable tone of voice. I didn't want to go on hearing the same message over and over again, so I didn't. In retrospect it all seems so stupid because I know that he loves both of our children equally, he was just really concerned about money at the time, only he chose a very immature way to deal with it.

Sometimes negotiation is a trial-and-error process. What works for one person in one situation will possibly not work for another person, even in the same situation. Keep a systematic record of what works and what doesn't work. A systematic record can reveal how we can better deal with difficult situations and/or difficult people. For example, when people who wanted to lose weight were asked to write down what they ate in the last week and then put on that same diet, they lost weight. Why? Because they forgot about a cookie that they ate or a snack they had. By keeping a systematic record you might find that the behavior that you find very troublesome happens a lot less frequently than you thought and the best strategy is to develop more tolerance. On the other hand, you may find that the behavior happens so frequently that you need to be more assertive and try a new strategy.

4. Six Positive Conflict Resolution Strategies

There are six strategies that can help all of the parties learn positive conflict resolution strategies and once learned, these strategies can help in all types of conflicts. These six strategies follow in the next sections.

4.1 Negotiate a good substantive, relationship, and process outcome

All negotiations have three parts: outcome, relationship, and process. Expert negotiators pay attention to each of these three highly important interrelated parts of the negotiation process. Expert negotiators also know that intervening in one part can change each of the other components.

The substantive outcome is made up of the details of the agreement that the parties reach. The relationship is the type of relationship that the parties will have during and after the negotiation, and the process is the method that the parties use to reach an agreement. For example, an ex-husband may end up getting his way about whether his son plays competitive hockey. However, if he forces this outcome on his ex-wife (the process), he may poison their relationship for years to come. On the other hand, if this couple went to mediation (the process), and were able to mutually agree that their son could play competitive hockey as long as he maintained his grades at school (the substantive outcome), the relationship between the ex-spouses could actually be improved because both parties would feel that their interests were taken into account and validated.

4.2 Develop a code of conduct

When I consult with organizations, one of the most successful interventions I use is to ask the team to develop a code of conduct. A code of conduct is acceptable norms of group behavior to which the participants agree upon via consensus. The team then has to commit to hold themselves accountable to the code of conduct that the team itself developed.

Likewise, developing a code of conduct for separating and divorcing couples can be especially helpful during the transition phase where the old family norms and standards do not seem to apply and where the new ones have not yet been developed. In terms of group process this is called forming, storming, and norming. The first stage is forming a new family which may mean becoming a family of three rather than a family of four or becoming a blended family. Storming refers to that period of time when the new family is trying to work out its own way of operating, and norming refers to the time after the new family has worked out and agreed to the norms under which it will operate. As you can imagine the storming period is the most unstable, as it is also the time where there will be the most jockeying for power. A sample code of conduct that was used by one of the families I interviewed appears in Sample 3.

4.3 Have productive family meetings

I have been teaching interest-based negotiation and facilitation skills for the past 24 years and have taught these skills to my children and my children have taught them to me. Although I had read a great deal about family meetings, I must admit that I had been reluctant to try them in our family as I felt that we already had quite enough structure in our lives; that is, until one day when we had a large enough problem that we didn't have much choice. At the time that the problem arose, my ex-wife and I had been separated for just over two years. The new

Sample 3
Muriel and Paul's Code of Conduct

Our children need to love, be loved, and have a close relationship with both parents.

We will not communicate indirectly with each other through our children.

We will not put each other down.

We will keep issues between us, between us.

If we run into any difficulties, either parent can ask for mediation and/or family counseling.

---

tradition for Easter was that the children spend Easter Saturday and Saturday night at their Mom's. My son and I would then pick up my daughter after church at 11:30 a.m. on Easter Sunday and then we would drive two hours to White Point Beach Lodge on Nova Scotia's beautiful south shore. The resort is exceptionally well run and there are many supervised activities for the children which give their parents time to relax and unwind undisturbed; a true break for both parents and children. There are several families who are friends of ours who also have a tradition of spending Easter at White Point which makes a great experience even better.

The problem one year was that the hours for the church service had changed and now the church service would end at 1:30 p.m. This meant that we would not arrive at White Point until 3:30. I suggested that we have a family meeting to discuss our options.

We first listed every option we could think of: postponing the trip to another weekend, Katie could miss church, we could go after church, or Katie could leave in the middle of the church service. Before we debated our options, I suggested that we develop criteria to help us evaluate our options.

I suggested that the most deserving family member should get to decide. As I had a pinched nerve in my neck, that would make me the most deserving. But I got voted down. Katie suggested that we have a debate and Andrew suggested listing the pros and cons of each option.

Andrew took the minutes of the meeting. I teach these skills to adults and it is a difficult skill set to learn. That he had this skill set so well developed truly blew me away. After discussing the various possibilities, we decided that the best option that would maximize the most interests would be to go to White Point and have Katie forego church. Katie was subsequently able to attend the Good Friday church concert with her Mom, and we were all happy. The meeting had gone so well, that we immediately decided to tackle a second issue, with Katie as the minute taker, on how we could not only have more fun as a family, but more adventure as well. Ten options were developed and the minutes for our family meetings kept in a journal, which from then on helped remind us of our commitments as well as act as a fascinating history of our deliberations as a family.

I must admit that I was surprised, the following week, when Katie called a family meeting about getting a dog. I called a family meeting about cleaning up after oneself, and Andrew asked for a family meeting about staying out later for special events such as his high school musical's cast party.

The family meetings have given us a forum where we can jointly and collaboratively work on solutions to family problems and challenges. Equally important, they are a vehicle where each of us can further develop our negotiating, debating, mediating, influencing, facilitating, and creative problem-solving skills. Since these are critical skills for both the home and the workplace, it is wise to start early. Sharing the responsibility for chairing the meetings and recording the minutes also helped each family member develop these essential skills.

Family meetings also provide the participants with a safe opportunity to offer feedback that is necessary to help the individuals and the family as a whole grow. For example, sometimes I have a short temper. When I display it, I have given the children permission to call me on it by saying "Temper, temper," or making a "T" sign with their hands to remind me to take a brief time-out, because they may see me starting to lose my temper before I do. This also demonstrates good modeling. If I am open to their feedback, it increases the likelihood that they will be open to mine. Lastly, it is important to note that family meetings cannot only be used to solve problems, they can also be used to make sure that the family capitalizes on all of the opportunities that are available such as learning to be assertive, respectful, and responsible, as well as learning how to have more fun and add more adventure and celebrations which are equally important. For more information on family meetings see Barbara Coloroso's book, *Kids are Worth it!*, (William Morrow, 2002).

4.3a Making sure that everyone gets a chance to talk

Some people are naturally more verbal and outgoing than others. One good way to make sure that everyone gets to talk, and is not interrupted when trying to talk is to get a tennis ball or something similar. The rule then is that only the person who has the ball gets to talk and as long as the person has the ball he or she can't be interrupted. If you have some rather long-winded family members, you may also need a rule that no one gets to talk for more than two or three minutes at a time. Using the ball is a small thing, but it is amazing how well it works.

4.3b Brainstorming and enhanced brainstorming

As discussed earlier in this book, the ground rules for brainstorming are that there is a set period of time, for example, 10 or 15 minutes, to say any idea that comes to mind with absolutely no criticism. Often an idea that seems ill conceived may be an innovative solution to a problem, which can lead to an innovative idea, or it can be combined with other ideas to help resolve a problem.

Even though we know the ground rules, many times we silently criticize someone else's suggestion. An innovative procedure that can help counterbalance this natural tendency is to use enhanced brainstorming. In enhanced brainstorming, there are two brainstorming sessions. The first one is to brainstorm creative options. The second brainstorming session is to invent different creative options to make each of the options from the first brainstorming session work, rather than to think about ways that they wouldn't work. Once again, no criticism is allowed in the second brainstorming session. This procedure helps us use brainstorming not only in the generation of ideas, but also in the implementation of ideas.

4.4 Negotiating clearly understood agreements

When negotiating with your ex-spouse or children, make sure you have clearly understood agreements. For example, in negotiating with my children, I often thought that I had a clear understanding of and commitment to our negotiated agreements when in fact the message had not registered with my children. Master negotiator Bill Frank has a formula that helps clarify our understanding of what the precise agreement is with our children. The formula is to repeat the agreement three times with three different points of emphasis: "Do you understand?," "Do you agree?," and "Are you committed?" By the time you have gone through this three times, each time asking for understanding, agreement, and commitment, they often get it; conversely, if they agree and understand, but are not committed, it is better to bring this issue out into the open, find out their reservations, which may in fact be valid, and process it, rather than assume you have agreement, understanding, and commitment, only to find out later that you did not.

The other classic technique is to ask the other party to summarize his or her understanding of the agreement and/or to get the agreement in writing. For example, Paula and Rob found that between their busy schedules and their children's busy schedules, it was sometimes hard to remember what their final agreements were. Even when they wrote down what they thought was the final agreement was in their day-timers, they would sometimes find that they each had different interpretations of what the agreement was. Paula suggested that they email each other a summary of their agreements right after they reached an agreement. At first Rob thought that this was just one more thing he had to do on top of an already long to-do list. However, he gave it a try and instead of being a time waster, it turned out to be a time saver because he and Paula had written records, they were more careful in making their agreements, and fewer issues had to be renegotiated.

4.5 Find the balance between firmness and flexibility

In my request for advice from others, I got a delightful letter that was full of wisdom from a divorced mother about how she effectively dealt with questions of body piercing and tattooing with one of her teenage daughters.

> I have three teenage daughter — yes, I accept your sympathies — and I am a divorced, single parent to boot.
>
> My 16-year-old decided she needed to get a belly button ring. I didn't want her to because of the health risk, the fad factor, and the waste of money.
>
> We discussed it, I voiced my concerns and we came up with this: She had to wait three months (fad factor), she had to pay for it all herself (I doubted she would spend the $50), and she had to go with her older sister to a registered tattoo/piercing parlor. She was OK with this. She waited the three months, saved her own money, researched a healthy, safe piercing place, and got her older sister to take her. I had to compromise — she wanted it — she had to compromise. It all turned out well.

Now, I have a 14-year-old who wants to get a tattoo on her chest! I say why, who will see it? CONCERN! Try to tell her when she gets old, it will look like a mole and she will have to stretch it out to even see what it is. (She didn't find this funny.) I again am concerned with fad factor, health factor, and waste of money. OK — same rules, three months, you pay, you get your older sister to go to a registered safe place [with you] to get it done. It has been six months now, and although she still talks about getting one, she hasn't saved a cent. I guess I get my wish on this one, so far.

4.6 Turn the conflict into a teachable moment

Teachable moments are those points in time where we have an opportunity to teach one of life's important lessons. When Shakespeare said "Ripeness is all," he was referring to the importance of timing. In other words, the time is ripe to teach one of life's most important lessons — the hard part is first being aware that we are in a teachable moment and second, having the wherewithal to say something that is coherent.

One of life's most important lessons is to realize that some things are better off not being negotiated. We also need to learn how to agree to disagree without becoming disagreeable, and learn that there are some things that we can't change and/or to learn to live with, and sometimes even to value diversity. For example, Rick reports that the one irresolvable issue between him and his ex-wife Abigail and their two children, Roger and Jessica, was the issue of how clean is clean.

> I grew up in a house that was crazy clean. My ex-wife also grew up in a house that was crazy clean. However, after we had children, Abigail felt that it was more important for her to spend time with the children than to have everything put away. While we were married, we compromised. We kept the downstairs picked up and the upstairs could look after itself. However after we set up our own households, that's when things really started to change. The children seemingly didn't have to pick up after themselves at all at their Mom's. Naturally their housekeeping standards started to deteriorate at my house as well. My son, Roger, especially, just threw things wherever he felt like it, and this drove me crazy. I tried talking to their mother to see if we could set a common standard at both houses and she wouldn't agree to even discuss it. It was her house and she was now an independent person. I said that we might

be teaching the children poor time management skills as the average adult spends two years of life looking for lost items. Her response was that I was being "anal-retentive." I finally figured out that she was using this issue to get back at me and that I was being set up to be the bad parent and she was setting herself up to be the good parent.

I felt caught; if I let it go, I became resentful of the time that I spent picking up after the children and I felt that they were learning a poor life lesson. I finally negotiated with my children what the minimal standard for picking up after oneself should be in our family. When they agreed that there should be a minimal standard,they also agreed that there should be a standard. In the end, we agreed that their bedroom was their room and only had to be picked up and vacuumed once a week. Anything left in any other part of the house was fair game to be confiscated and put in the basement for a period of one week. We also had a very good family meeting where we discussed that it was natural for people to have different standards. The perfect analogy is that different teachers have different standards for spelling, grammar, neatness, and quietness in the classroom. Roger and Jessica had learned to accommodate their teachers and learning when to and how to accommodate was an important life lesson; a lesson that also applied to how clean is clean and how neat in neat in their two homes.

As parents we are, at all times, modeling either good or bad conflict resolution for our children, and in most cases our children are perceptive enough to notice how their parents treat each other even when the parents don't think so. Therefore, we must be very careful about what we are teaching our children both directly by what we say, but more importantly indirectly by the examples we set. There are also times when we have to and need to teach our children that some differences can not be and possibly should not be negotiated.

8

How to Negotiate with a Difficult Ex-Spouse

Ninety percent of our stress is a result of dealing ineffectively with people we find difficult. These are the people to whom we can get emotionally hooked. Often it seems that the harder we try to extricate ourselves from these situations, the more entangled we become.

Negotiating effectively with difficult people requires that we do not get enmeshed, or if we do get enmeshed, that we quickly extricate ourselves. All of this requires a great deal of self-control. Therefore, the first thing you need to do in dealing with a difficult person is not to control the difficult person's behavior, but control your own. For the purposes of this book, self-control can be defined as:

- The ability to keep your emotions in check and not let them override or interfere with your judgment.

- The ability not to overly personalize the situation or the behavior of the other party and stay focused on those things that are truly important.

- The ability to make rational decisions to behave in a particular way in spite of strong emotional feelings to behave in the opposite way.

1. Why Do Difficult People Behave in Difficult Manners?

Difficult people behave in difficult manners because they have learned that doing so keeps others off-balance and incapable of effective action. In order to help determine which type of response you want to make to the difficult behavior, you first need to describe as specifically as possible what the other party does that makes it difficult for you to negotiate effectively. For example, some of the behaviors that the people I interviewed found difficult in their ex-spouses were: aggressiveness, passivity, passive-aggressiveness, loudness, swearing, shouting, lying, not listening, name-calling, constantly interrupting, threatening to call a lawyer, belittling, withholding relevant information, abusing exes in public, being overly persistent, not letting exes speak, and negotiating behind exes' backs through other people.

In addition to carefully observing how the other party behaves, you need to figure out what he or she needs or wants. Some of the things difficult people want are control, power, attention, to be right, and status. By carefully figuring out what the other party wants, you will be in a better position to negotiate effectively with him or her because it will be easier for you to give the person some of what he or she wants, which will make it much less likely that you will get emotionally hooked.

Protecting yourself from getting emotionally hooked and getting yourself unhooked once you get hooked is one of the major focuses of this chapter. This is called changing the viewing, which means that, where appropriate, we change how we view the situation. One way to change the viewing is to see that difficult people and difficult situations are a true test of your negotiating and influencing skills. These situations will also provide you with one of the best sources of information of what we need to change in order to negotiate more effectively. Therefore, in order to improve your negotiating skills and your self-control, you need to master the eight essential skills in the following sections.

2. The Power of an Accurate Diagnosis

In medicine, a correct diagnosis is half the cure. Therefore, just like in medicine, it is imperative that you accurately diagnose difficult situations before you try to treat them.

There are basically two types of difficult people. The majority (96 percent) of difficult people are situationally difficult. They are suffering from exceptional stress, they are in a difficult situation, they do not have the skills to negotiate more effectively, and/or they do not perceive that they have any viable options. Once viable options are put on the table, their behavior ceases to be difficult.

The other type is the four percent of the population that are difficult across almost all situations. These people behave as they do because it works for them — that is, they get what they want frequently enough to reinforce their negative behavior, and they have had years of practice in their families of origin and subsequent practice on countless unsuspecting strangers.

Therefore, as a negotiator, you have to make an accurate diagnosis. There are two types of errors commonly made when making this type of diagnosis. First, if we diagnose a situationally difficult person as being a perennially difficult person, we risk giving up prematurely or behaving in a difficult manner ourselves, and thus ending up with a self-fulfilling prophecy. For example, John's story:

> I thought my ex-spouse was being difficult. I overreacted and behaved in a difficult manner myself. She reacted to my being difficult and became more difficult. I reacted to her becoming more difficult by becoming more adversarial, and so on, until it became a self-fulfilling prophecy. If only I had asked the right question or shared a piece of information that I chose to withhold, the outcome of the negotiation would have been entirely different — maybe even entirely satisfactory.

The other type of error we can make is continually trying to negotiate with people who will not or cannot change. We fall into the trap of blaming ourselves and thinking that if only we were more skillful, things would be different; we continually ask advice from our friends and confidants, until our friends and confidants start to label us as difficult because we hang in there for years after we should have quit. Finally, we realize that we have used up years of emotional energy and have received nothing in return. In cases like this, learning when not to negotiate and go with our BATNA (Best Alternative To A Negotiated Agreement) instead of trying to negotiate is one of the most important lessons that we can learn.

2.1 Labeling

Once we have labeled someone, we tend to believe that the label itself is true. For example, if we label someone as an opponent, we are less likely to observe any un-opponent-like behavior such as an invitation to engage in more cooperative problem solving.

We may prematurely label a person because we lack critical information. At one time or another, all of us have been labeled negatively and unfairly by someone who did not fully understand the situation. I call this phenomenon premature labeling. We dislike it when it happens to us, and we should be careful not to do it to others. Not only is it unfair, it also makes us less effective as negotiators. There are four rules of thumb which can help us avoid premature labeling:

1. Have I observed the same behavior in three similar situations? The first time it may have been an accident; the second time it starts to look like a pattern; the third time it probably is a pattern.

2. Is the other party experiencing exceptional stress? For example, let's say that you have observed your ex-spouse behaving in a difficult manner recently in three similar situations. However, you have also heard that he or she is under considerable pressure at work or is experiencing financial difficulties because the economy has worsened or the demand for the product that he or she sells has dried up. Therefore, your ex-spouse may very well be suffering from situational stress, and that stress may be the root cause of his or her behavior.

3. Am I experiencing situational stress? There have been times when each of us has been under enough stress that it has influenced us to see other people's behavior more negatively than it really is.

4. If you have observed the same negative behavior on three separate occasions, and if the other party is not suffering from too much stress, and you are not suffering from too much stress, there is still one more question you have to answer before labeling the other person's behavior as difficult. The question is: "Have I had an adult-to-adult conversation with the other party in an effort to resolve the problem and improve the situation?" There are times when the other party may not realize that his or her behavior is causing a problem for someone else, and we may be able to negotiate a good solution to the problem during this adult-to-adult conversation.

You will be in a much better position to negotiate with your ex-spouse when you can see clearly both your behavior and theirs. An excellent way to do this is to   describe in writing how you perceive the problem. For example, Joan describes her problems with her ex-husband Randy as follows.

> Randy is a lawyer and he never learned to leave his profession at work. He always has to win his case whether that case is at work or at home, with me or with the children. With almost every issue or every discussion I felt like I was on the witness stand, and he played both of the role of judge and prosecutor. He could never agree to disagree, and he kept trying to wear me and the children down. As a result, they told me that they don't enjoy going over to his house. When I try to talk to him about this, he accuses me of trying to poison his relationship with the children.

The next step is to write down as clearly as possible how you perceive that the other person sees the problem. This is important because "You are not in a position to change someone's mind or their perception of the situation, unless you first know what their perception of the problem is." For example, when I interviewed Randy about the problems he and Joan were having, he stated the following.

> Joan is a very good mother, but I find her too aggressive when it comes to making decisions about our children. She wants me to be an equal co-parent only when it comes to child support. She does not keep me informed about what is going on in the children's lives, although I do my best to share my observations and concerns. Once I got into a new relationship it only got worse. I think she is punishing me for getting on with my life and that she is trying to live vicariously through the children because she hasn't much of a life outside of them and her work.

Given that Joan and Randy have made the above assumptions, it is no wonder they have trouble understanding and communicating with each other.

An excellent way to understand what is actually going on is to actually write out a piece of the dialogue you had with the difficult person. One approach to this is to divide a page in half by drawing a vertical line down the middle, and in the left-hand column, write down each party's initials to identify each person and then write out their corresponding dialogue, Then go back and write down in the right-hand column what you thought and/or felt at each part of the dialogue. This exercise is guaranteed to help you gain insight into the behavior of both participants. Armed with this insight, you are in a position to negotiate more effectively. An example of this technique using the case of Joan and Randy appears in Sample 4.

Sample 4
Original Dialogue

> **Randy:** I have this big deadline for a case that has gotten terribly complicated. I wonder if you could keep the kids Friday night and I will pick them up first thing Saturday morning?
>
> **Joan:** Well you may not realize it, but I have a life too and I have plans to go out with my friends on Friday.
>
> **Randy:** I know you have a life, but I am really jammed up. Can you hire a babysitter and I will pay for it?
>
> **Joan:** So what are you teaching our children about being respectful of your commitments and having a work/life balance? It was bad enough that you always put your work ahead of me, now you are doing the same thing with our children.
>
> **Randy:** It is my work that has allowed you to stay in the only house the children have ever known.

It is easy to see how things escalated from reading the dialogue in Sample 5. However, when you look at the feelings and thoughts behind the dialogue as we do in the next sample, both Randy and Joan have more in common than first appears on the surface of the dialogue. Once they share some of their inner thoughts and feelings and if, and it is a big if, they listen respectfully to each other, they have a chance not only to have a better understanding and hence a better relationship, they will be better role models for their children. If either or both parties cannot listen to each other respectfully, then the best strategy is to minimize the damage and learn how to negotiate without increasing the muscle level.

You can try this technique out for yourself in Exercise 14.

3. The Power of Perspective Management

Perspective management is our first line of defense against losing our self-control in dealing with difficult people. Perspective management protects us from becoming emotionally hooked, or if we get hooked, it

Sample 5
Dialogue with Negative Thoughts and Feelings

Randy: I have this big deadline for a case that has gotten terribly complicated. I wonder if you could keep the kids Friday night and I will pick them up first thing Saturday morning?

She has to say "yes". I am under so much pressure. She has to!

Joan: Well you may not realize it, but I have a life too and I have plans to go out with my friends on Friday.

Here we go again. His needs are always more important than mine. Well not this time you inconsiderate "$&*@#"

Randy: I know you have a life, but I am really jammed up. Can you hire a ... baby sitter and I will pay for it?

Here she goes again.

Joan: So what are you teaching our children about being respectful of your commitments and having a work/life balance. It was bad enough that you always put your work ahead of me, now you are doing the same thing with our children.

So you want me to find you a babysitter. This proves that you still think your time and your priorities are more important than mine.

Randy: It is my work that has allowed you to stay in the only house the children have ever known.

Give me a break. Can't you see how much I have sacrificed for you and the kids?

helps us keep our psychological distance. Sylvia's story illustrates the concept of perspective management. Sylvia realized that there were adult issues and child issues and through perspective management was able to keep them separate.

Sylvia and Jeff had two children; Megan, age 12 and Zack, age 9. Both children were excellent students, musicians, and athletes. However, one day, the children came to Sylvia and complained that their dad, Jeff, wasn't very understanding. Upon further probing, Sylvia found that the children didn't think that their father could emphasize with their feelings. Sylvia was then thrown into a dilemma. One of the reasons that she and Jeff divorced was, at least as far as she was concerned, Jeff was emotionally tone-deaf. When they married, Sylvia had always assumed that

Dialogue with Neutral to Positive Thoughts and Feelings

Randy: I have this big deadline for a case that has gotten terribly complicated. I wonder if you could help me?

Boy I hope she will be reasonable this time.

Joan: What did you have in mind?

I think I will get scammed again, but I will listen respectfully to what he wants.

Randy: If the children could stay with you Friday night, and I could pick them up first thing Saturday morning, it would be great.

Joan: I have plans to go out with friends on Friday.

Randy: If I hired a babysitter and took care of dinner would that work for you?

That's a more reasonable request.

Joan: If you can hire a babysitter and take care of dinner, it would be OK.

What a relief, I owe you one.

Randy: Not only will I take care of dinner and hire a babysitter, I want you to know how much I appreciate this and I definitely owe you one.

---

she could teach Jeff to be more empathic. At this point, she said, "I don't know if he doesn't want to learn or he can't learn, but the end result is the same." The dilemma for Sylvia was that she wanted to support her children and in this regard she wanted to validate their perceptions that their father had a hard time being empathic. On the other hand, she didn't want to denigrate Jeff in the eyes of their children.

Sylvia turned to family therapist and relationship expert Nina Woulff for help.

A proven method to help you regain your perspective after you have lost it is to analyze how your core values and your core beliefs have been psychologically hooked and to examine where your core values and beliefs work for you and where they work against you.

Exercise 14
Actual Dialogue

What my ex-spouse said:

What I said:

What my ex-spouse said:

What I said:

What my ex-spouse said:

What I said:

What my ex-spouse said:

What I said:

Exercise 15
The Power of Perspective Management

Describe three situations in which you successfully used or plan to successfully use perspective management to help you negotiate effectively with your ex-partner.

1.

2.

3.

Exercise 16
Using Perspective Management More Effectively

In reviewing the above three situations, what have you learned about perspective management that will help you to keep your perspective and negotiate more effectively with your ex-partner in the future?

4. The Power of Core Values and Core Beliefs

In negotiating and in dealing with difficult people, we frequently hear phrases such as: "She presses my hot buttons every time; so I continually lose it with her!" The problem with the phrase "hot buttons" is that we rarely stop to think what this phrase refers to.

The phrase "hot buttons" refers to your core values and core beliefs. Once your core values and/or your beliefs are hooked, you are likely to:

1. Lose your perspective.

2. Become angry, hurt, or defensive.

3. Make non-vigilant decisions (underreact by not saying or doing what needs to be said or done).

4. Make hyper-vigilant decisions (over-react by saying or doing things that should not be said or done).

All of the above will cause you to negotiate less effectively than you would like. In learning to negotiate effectively, there are two basic points to remember: Keep your perspective, and keep your self-control. There are also two essential points to remember in order to negotiate a successful outcome: know what your core values and core beliefs are, and know where your core values and core beliefs work for you and know where they work against you.

The first step is to define what core values and core beliefs are. Core values are deeply held values that govern how we behave across a great many situations. Core values are powerful because they generate feelings, thoughts, and behavior. A negative example of how Kevin allowed his ex-wife to use his core value of being a nice guy against him follows.

> All the time we were married, I was the principal bread-winner. My ex-wife, Darla, had a small catering business on the side. During the marriage we both worked, catering small functions on the weekends, and this was one of the things we had in common. After a very difficult separation, Darla and I agreed that each of us would have our two children 50 percent of the time. Darla stayed in our house and I moved in with my mother. Not only did Darla not look for full-time work, she let the catering business run itself into the ground. In the meantime 70 percent of my disposable income was going to Darla so she could

keep the children in their "proper" home. She kept telling me that they had enough to adjust to without having to move and I bought into that. Three years later my mother has moved into a nursing home, Darla is still getting 70 percent of my income, I have zero disposable income, and my lawyer tells me it may take years to change things because we now have a three-year precedent, all because I felt so guilty.

Core values can also be positive, as in the story on the evening news about a 16-year-old in the Midwest. His father had recently died of Lou Gehrig's disease. His family donated their family van, equipped with a wheelchair lift, to a charitable car auction. The funds raised from the car auction would go to medical research. The young man had worked all summer long to finance the purchase of his first car, which he had planned to buy at the same auction. The bidding had started on his family's van. A woman who also had Lou Gehrig's disease bid on the van. Unfortunately, she had to drop out after the bidding reached the limit of her funds. The young man in our story noticed this and continued the bidding, sacrificing the money he had earned for his own car so the woman would be able to have transportation. Obviously, the positive core value in this case was altruism.

How do core values affect the negotiating process? As negotiators, we need to know what our core values are so that we can develop control over them rather than letting our core values control us. For example, perhaps one of your core values is being polite, and your ex-spouse is rude to you. If you automatically become angry and attack your ex-spouse without first thinking about an appropriate strategy, your core value of politeness has been hooked, and you become a reactive negotiator rather than a proactive one.

How do we discover what our core values and core beliefs are? One of the best methods of discovering what are your core values are is to keep a log of the difficult people you encounter at home, at work, or in the community. For each episode you encounter with a difficult person and/or a difficult situation, write a brief description in your log. At the end of your description, identify the core value or values that were hooked for you. Tony's example follows.

My ex-wife still expects me to be empathic to her problems and concerns even though she is almost never empathic with my concerns. For example, while we were married my mother died, but she only mentioned it once. After we were divorced, I had to go in for surgery. After the operation, she never asked how I was. On the other hand, when things go badly for her, she expects a sympathetic ear. This always surprises me and I am surprised that I am surprised because it is such a consistent pattern and was one of the main reasons for my wanting the divorce in the first place.

What were the core values/core beliefs that were being hooked on Tony's part?

1. Fairness/reciprocity.

2. People should be caring and thoughtful and when they are not, it's wrong.

Once you have analyzed your core values and core beliefs, you are ready to move on to step two where you carefully examine where your core values work for you and where they work against you. In the above case, Tony learned to see that one of the reasons that he had so many loyal and long-term friends was because he was caring, empathic, and loyal. What he had to learn was to be more selective about where to apply those values.

There will also be times when we have analyzed a situation and we just can't seem to pinpoint the core value. Often this happens; it is because we are too close to the situation. Explaining the situation to a trusted and insightful friend will help us to see the previously hidden core value.

Core beliefs are very similar to core values. Psychologist Albert Ellis based a great deal of his school of psychotherapy, Rational-Emotive Therapy, on helping people to examine their core beliefs and decide more consciously whether or not they apply in specific situations. For example, three of the primary self-defeating beliefs that Ellis named are: I must be perfect; people should approve of me; and life must be fair.

Think about a situation in which you were emotionally hooked. Then fill out the Core Beliefs Identification in Exercise 19. If you fill out the form for situations in which you were emotionally hooked in the past and/or for new situations when they arise, the chances are good that you will see that the same core beliefs keep turning up.

Awareness is the first step along the road to positive change.

Remember the last time you felt bad about something; angry, jealous, and resentful of your ex-partner. What were you telling yourself? In the exercise, you are going to challenge the destructive self-talk that caused you those difficulties. Fill in the rest of the form for the event

Exercise 17
Identification of Core Values

1. In the space provided, briefly describe a situation that was difficult for you.

   Was there a core value(s) that had you hooked in this particular negotiation? If so, please name the core value(s):

   _____, _____,
   _____.

   If you need help in identifying the core value(s), who would be a good person(s) to contact _____,
   _____?

   Last, how do you need to modify the way you use this core value to insure that it will continue to work for you in those situations where it should work for you, and not use the core value(s) in situations where it has worked against you?

2. Briefly describe a second situation that was difficult for you.

   Was there a core value(s) that had you hooked in this particular negotiation? If so, please name the core value(s):

   _____, _____,
   _____.

   If you need help in identifying the core value(s), who would be a good person(s) to contact _____,
   _____? Last, how do you need to modify the way you use this core value to ensure that it will continue to work for you in those situations where it should work for you, and not use the core value(s) in situations where it has worked against you?

3. Briefly describe a third situation that was difficult for you.

   Was there a core value(s) that had you hooked in this particular negotiation? If so, please name the core value(s):

   _____, _____,
   _____.

   If you need help in identifying the core value(s), who would be a good person(s) to contact _____,
   _____?

   Last, how do you need to modify the way you use this core value to insure that it will continue to work for you in those situations where it should work for you, and not use the core value(s) in situations where it has worked against you?

Exercise 18
Modifying Core Values/Core Beliefs

1. List the core values you have identified that need to be modified.

2. How do they need to be modified so you can negotiate more effectively?

you have just thought about. Write down your self-destructive talk in your own words. It may well include self-condemnation and be full of what you think you should or ought to do.

5. The Power of Effective Anger Management

One of my favorite expressions is, "I gave the best speech I regretted when I was angry." Likewise, each of us can cite examples of situations in which we allowed ourselves to become so angry that we damaged the negotiation to the point where the outcome of the negotiation was that we got less out of it than we could have or should have, and/or we damaged a relationship that was important to us. In cases like this, too much anger and/or too much uncontrolled anger resulted in our making non-vigilant or hyper-vigilant decisions, which negatively affected both the process of the negotiation and its outcome.

Statistical research indicates that one-third of all automobile accidents occur when the driver is angry. Inappropriate expressions of anger contribute not only to car accidents, but also to ruined negotiations. It is imperative, therefore, that good negotiators know how to both manage and express anger appropriately.

Some of the techniques that were already discussed that aid in effective anger management are: perspective management, talking out the problem with someone outside of the negotiation, taking a cooling-off break, and/or writing down actions to be taken at each muscle level so we will not escalate too soon or too quickly.

The Anger Management Form in Exercise 20 can also help us process our anger in a way that is more likely to be effective. This form contains three important questions.

Following is an example of how this technique was used. A blank form is included on the download kit that comes with this book for you to use.

Exercise 19
Core Beliefs Identification

Example: My Self-Defeating Belief Is That Life Isn't Fair

The event: We separated ostensibly because I had an affair. The truth is that the marriage had been dead for years and we stayed together for the sake of our children.

However, I felt so guilty that I gave my ex-wife 70 percent of my income even though we have joint parenting. My ex-wife still lives in our house and does not work. I moved in with my mother who lives in the country, 30 miles out of town. Now that our three sons are older, they want to spend more and more time in the city and less and less time in the country. So I do all of the driving back and forth and most of the driving to and from the children's activities. In other words, I do most of the parenting and I am the principal breadwinner. I love spending time with our children but I am broke and exhausted most of the time and my ex-wife is living in comparative luxury.

What I felt: Dejected and depressed. At this rate I will never be able to have my own home again and I am playing a less active role in my children's lives than I would like.

What I was telling myself: The situation is hopeless.

What it made me do: I started spending more and more time doing nothing constructive.

What my self-defeating belief was: Life sucks and it isn't going to change.

Now challenge that self-talk, reinterpret it by exchanging the shoulds and oughts for preference. Talk to yourself about what you can learn from experience. Tell yourself that you can behave differently next time.

I can fix up the farm because at some point my mother is going to sell it. At that point I will either keep it or sell it. I will spend some of my time on the farm getting into top notch physical shape. Lastly, I will make sure that our boys have Sunday dinner at the farm at least twice a month. They can spend the night and I will drive them to school in the morning and that way I will have quality time both during dinner and in the drive back to the city.

Fill in the table below with alternative constructive self-talk and the consequences that could have resulted.

My constructive self-talk would be: Fixing up the farm is much better than sitting around feeling sorry for myself.

My feelings would be: I would feel that I am in control of a major portion of my life.

My constructive actions will be: I will join Weight Watchers™, and either develop a fitness program that I can do by myself on the farm, or I will join a gym. I need to lose 30 to 40 pounds and I will get a good scale that will allow me to measure my progress. I will also endeavor to eat more healthy food and have a healthy dinner on Sundays with leftovers that I can take to work which will save me enough money to pay for Weight Watchers™. When I no longer need Weight Watchers™, I will invest the money I save in used exercise equipment for the farm or join a gym, or both.

In the end, changing his negative beliefs and negative self-talk paid huge dividends for Tony. He lost 30 pounds. The farm looks 100 percent better and he met a wonderful woman at the gym. Now her children join them for Sunday night dinners and Tony has a warm feeling of having a home. There are also enough children around so everyone wants to spend more time at the farm because they now have enough good friends that they can do things together. Now it is your turn to explore your core beliefs.

Craig came to see me because he was in a moral dilemma. He felt that his ex-wife Suzanne had unfairly made decisions about their daughter, Paulette, without consulting him. For example, one day when Suzanne was dropping Paulette off at the house, Suzanne casually asked Paulette in front of Craig if Paulette would like to be confirmed this month or next. Craig was shocked because he and Suzanne had never discussed their eight-year-old daughter's getting confirmed and this constituted a major decision, and he wasn't even part of the decision. If he had been asked, Craig would have preferred that Paulette get confirmed (or not) when she was a teenager and could better determine for herself if she wanted to get confirmed. Since Paulette wanted to get confirmed, and Suzanne and Paulette had already decided that it would be this month or next, if Craig made a fuss, it could turn Paulette against him. If he did nothing it condoned Suzanne's behavior of not including him and it set a terrible precedent for the future.

Craig wisely decided that this was a no-win situation for him and he attended the confirmation ceremony in good faith. He also felt that when Paulette was older she could still make an independent decision about religion. The thing that Craig felt that he must do, however, was negotiate with Suzanne about developing some standards or guidelines as to which decisions each parent should make independently and which decisions should be treated as shared decisions. The problem was that Suzanne did not want to negotiate any kind of a guideline that could fence her in. I advised Craig that one of the best ways to process his anger effectively was to use the Anger Management Form.

Craig's responses to the questions in Exercise 20 were as follows:

Exercise 20
Anger Management Form

1. How intense are you going to allow your anger to become?

   I asked Craig to imagine a scale running from one to 10. If the 1 point on the scale represents absolute calm, and the 10 point on the scale represents absolute rage, at the point Craig found out that he was not part of the decision-making process regarding his daughter's confirmation, Craig said that he was at an eight or nine. The scaling question clearly gives you a great deal of information about how angry you are. It also enables you to rank the degree of anger relative to specific events and to measure changes in the degree of anger over time.

2. How long are you going to stay angry?

   Craig answered, "I have been upset about not being consulted in my daughter's confirmation for over a year. I know it is foolish for me to continue to be upset, but I just can't seem to shake it. I feel that I was treated very poorly." I asked Craig how much longer he wanted to stay angry, and he said that he wanted to get over his angry feelings immediately. This told me that the time was right for Craig to let go of his angry feelings; we just needed to find the right mechanism to help him do it. I hoped that the next question would be that mechanism.

3. How are you going to use your anger constructively?

   Craig decided that he would become much more proactive in negotiating agreements and he would keep as detailed records of their agreements as possible through emails. In other words, Craig developed a strategy to use the energy behind his anger constructively. Ruminating about the unfair way he was treated was a negative use of Craig's time and energy, whereas developing a proactive agreement strategy was a positive use of Craig's time and energy.

Another way we can use the concept of anger management positively as a negotiator is to decide ahead of time what social role we want to take on as we negotiate.

5. The Power of Role Selection

We assume different roles all the time. In any given day you might play the role of a professional, a husband or wife, a parent, son or daughter, coach, girl scout leader, president of the PTA, etc. When we assume each particular role, we take on certain characteristics of that role. For example, when my daughter suffered an eye accident while we were in a store, I saw my wife assume the role of physician, which is her occupation. Lynn calmly told the sales staff at the store to call the local children's hospital to alert them that we were bringing in a child whose eye had been severely traumatized. Lynn then calmly turned to me, and asked if I thought I would be able to drive to the hospital. She remained calm during the entire trip to the hospital. As soon as Lynn turned our daughter over to the emergency room physician, she broke down. At that point, she allowed herself to leave the physician role and become Katie's mother.

When we can consciously choose what role we want to take during a negotiation, it gives us the power to select how we want to behave in the negotiation. It is important to look at times when we have used positive roles as frames of reference to help us negotiate more effectively. I would like you now to think of at least one watershed moment when you were surprised at how well you maintained your self-control.

For example, after my daughter's eye accident, I negotiated with the department store vice-president regarding their safety standards. The vice-president said, "As parents, we are all responsible for our children. As a parent, you are partially responsible for her accident." The parent in me wanted to throttle the man. However, in the negotiator role, I was able to say, "If I had left my daughter unattended at an elevator or escalator, I could see how I would have been responsible; however, one would assume that one was in a relatively safe environment in the main aisle of your store. If you do not do everything in your power to protect the children who enter your store, I will have no other choice but to go to the press because if another accident were to occur and I did not do everything I could do to prevent it, I would feel that I was partly responsible."

When a friend of mine asked me what role I was taking on, I really had to stop and think about it. Then it hit me: The role I was taking on was that of a strong advocate for my beliefs. What I need to be absolutely clear on is where this role works for me and where it works against me. Sometime I advocate for issues that waste a lot of energy and generate a ton of stress in regard to issues that are not any of my business or issues where the transaction cost of being in the negotiation outweigh the benefit.

Just as it is important to be able to look at situations in which we can use positive roles as frames of reference to help us negotiate more effectively, it is also important to look at situations in which we have inadvertently fallen into roles that prevent us from negotiating effectively. For example, at a workshop I was teaching for the government, one of the participants made a negative and unjustified comment against a

Exercise 21
Self-Control

1. Describe a negotiation in which you demonstrated excellent self-control. What role were you playing in the situation that helped you maintain good self-control?

2. Describe a second negotiation in which you demonstrated excellent self-control. What role were you playing in the situation that helped you maintain good self-control?

3. Describe a third negotiation in which you demonstrated excellent self-control. What role were you playing in the situation that helped you maintain good self-control?

Exercise 22
Identification of Positive Roles

At this point, you have identified several situations in which you demonstrated excellent self-control in selected negotiations. You have also identified the roles you were playing in these negotiations that helped you maintain good self-control. In the space below, make a list of the positive roles that you can use on a more conscious and consistent basis to help you negotiate more effectively in the future:

a. _____

b. _____

c. _____

particular group of citizens. I lost my cool and called him on his remark in front of the other participants. I fell out of the teacher/facilitator role and into the role of irate citizen. A more effective negotiator/teacher/facilitator would have addressed the matter in private with the person.

A colleague of mine states that she never loses her sense of calm as a negotiator in public. She feels she has developed an excellent professional role to help her be effective in her professional life. She feels that she does "lose it" too frequently in her home life. In our interview, she stated that it is easier for her to lose self-control in the family. She has chosen to keep a log at home, to help her learn to be as effective a negotiator at home as she is at work.

Exercise 23
Self-Control Log

In the spaces below, briefly describe three incidents in which you did not demonstrate good self-control. After you have finished describing each situation, analyze it to determine how the role you played in each of the situations prevented you from maintaining your self-control.

a. _____

b. _____

c. _____

Exercise 24
Improving Self-Control

1. Describe a negotiation in which you demonstrated poor self-control with your ex-spouse. What role were you playing in the situation that prevented you from maintaining good self-control?

2. Describe a second negotiation in which you demonstrated poor self-control with your ex-spouse. What role were you playing in the situation that prevented you from maintaining good self-control?

3. Describe a third negotiation in which you demonstrated poor self-control with your ex-spouse. What role were you playing in the situation that prevented you from maintaining good self-control?

Exercise 25
Identifying Negative Roles

At this point, you have identified several situations in which you were not able to demonstrate good self-control in selected negotiations. You have also identified the roles you were playing in these negotiations that prevented you from maintaining good self-control. In the space below, please list the negative roles that you played:

a. _____

b. _____

c. _____

In order to negotiate more effectively in the future, you need to make a conscious effort not to fall into these roles.

6. The Power of Doing the Unexpected

When I was growing up in San Francisco, my grandmother and I frequently went exploring. One of my favorite places was Chinatown. It was on one of our trips to Chinatown that I discovered a Chinese finger trap. This toy is a narrow tube made out of straw reeds. You insert a finger in one end and invite an unsuspecting friend to put a finger in the opposite end. Each person then tries to pull their finger out of the tube. The more you pull, the harder it is to get your finger out because pulling causes the tube to become narrower and tighter. The most common reaction is to pull harder, which pulls the tube tighter still. It is only when one person does the unexpected, pushing their finger into the tube instead of pulling out, that the tube becomes wide enough to release both fingers.

Often, it turns out that doing the unexpected helps to disarm the difficult person with whom you are dealing. An example of this would be apologizing to a belligerent ex-spouse when he or she is expecting that you will become belligerent in return. Jay Carter, in his book entitled *Nasty People: How to Stop Being Hurt By Them Without Becoming One of Them*, (McGraw Hill, 2003), gives another example: A woman had been dominated by her husband for years. By passively condoning his domination, the wife reinforced the very behavior she wanted to change. In the latest round of negotiations, the wife wanted to enroll in an evening course in psychology. The husband said, "If you take that course, I'll divorce you!" The wife's usual reply would have been to not take the course. This time, however, she replies, "I love you; I do not want a divorce; however, I am going to take this course because it interests me very much. If you want a divorce, you will have to file for it." In this case, the wife did the unexpected. She didn't take the bait, get hysterical, and say, "How can you treat me this way?" Instead, she calmly told her husband that she loved him and did not want to get a divorce. She also told him that she was going to take the course and that if he wanted a divorce, it was his prerogative to file for one.

The "change-first principle" states that if you want to change some-one else's behavior or your relationship with that person, you have to change your own behavior first. In the literature on Brief Solution-Focused Therapy, this principle is stated as, "If it is working, do more of the same; if it isn't working, do something different."

6.1 The law of choice

The law of choice states that we always have a choice. We can always either change the doing, that is changing our behavior or the other person's behavior, or we can change the viewing; the way we view or perceive the situation. For example, Rebecca always wanted her ex-husband Rob to be more empathic and understanding of her feelings. However, rightly or wrongly, even after years of marital counseling, Rob was never empathic enough for Rebecca. At this point Rebecca and Rob separated and subsequently divorced.

However, just because they divorced, the issue did not go away and Rebecca still was angry about and felt badly about the fact that Rob couldn't or wouldn't be more empathic of the way she felt. I asked Rebecca if she had more influence over Rob when they were married or now that they are divorced. Rebecca answered that she had more influence over Rob's behavior when they were married. So if she couldn't get him to change his behavior when they were married, what was the likelihood or probability that she could get him to change his behavior now? Rebecca answered that it was slim to nonexistent. I then suggested that since Rebecca could not change the doing (the behavior), she could change the viewing. Intrigued, she asked me how. I suggest that she change her self-talk around the issue of Rob being more empathic. For example, she could tell herself how grateful she is that she and Rob have three wonderful and healthy children and how thankful she is to have empathic friends. The other choice she has is to look for a more empathic future partner when and if she decides that she wants to form a new relationship.

Exercise 26
Applying the Doing versus Viewing Principle in Your Own Life

1. What is the most important change you would like your ex-spouse/ partner to make?

   I would like my ex-spouse to be more _____ or less

   _____.

2. How realistic is it?

   If your spouse didn't change in the direction or the degree that you wanted him or her to change when you were married, how realistic is it that he or she will change his or her behavior now? Rate from 0 to 99 percent. _____

3 If you can't change the doing of your ex-spouse's/partner's behavior, how can you change the viewing?

   "Doing the unexpected," "The change-first principle," and "If it isn't working do something different," all have a common element. That element is changing a behavior pattern. When the old pattern no longer works, try a new pattern that does. In order to do this more frequently, we have to be aware of when we are at a "choice point" -- those critical points in a negotiation in which, if we choose to do something different, the negotiation will move forward towards a settlement; while more of the same behavior will continue the old pattern, lead to breaking off the negotiation, to an impasse, or the escalation of a fight.

My ex-husband Richard has a very short temper. He also tends to be dogmatic and often tries to browbeat me into seeing things his way. When he would call and try to browbeat me, I learned to do the unexpected by remarking on the 80 percent of the time that we were co-parenting very effectively and thanking him for helping to make this possible. He usually calmed right down after that.

Exercise 27
The Power of Doing the Unexpected

Describe a situation in which you used the power of the unexpected effectively.

7. The Power of Resiliency

Even the best negotiators make mistakes. However, one of the factors that best differentiates effective negotiators from their less effective counterparts is the way they deal with their mistakes. Effective negotiators have more resiliency; they accept that they are human and not perfect. They then turn their mistakes into learning opportunities, and subsequently have a shorter recovery time before returning to full effectiveness. Recovery time is the time that it takes a person to recover his or her equilibrium after a difficult negotiation. For example, we can go around and beat ourselves up mentally for the next five minutes, five days, five months, or the next five years; or we can ask ourselves what we learned from the negotiation and/or specify what we would do differently if we were to renegotiate that same negotiation.

When we get mentally beaten up or emotionally hooked by a difficult person, or if we feel we have made an important mistake in a negotiation, we may lose control over the process and/or the outcome. There is, however, one thing that we do have absolute control over, and that is the amount of time it takes us to recover.

By comparing the recovery time for Person A and Person B, we see that person A allows himself or herself to become more stressed and to stay stressed longer than person B. There are several proven techniques that we can use to get ourselves unhooked and to recover more quickly. Among the techniques previously covered in this chapter that can aid in recovery time are: accurate diagnosis, understanding core values and core beliefs, effective anger management, and the power of keeping things in perspective.

When these techniques do not work, there is another approach you can take if you have become emotionally hooked: You can turn

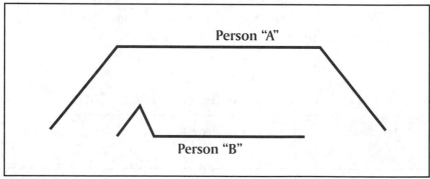

Figure 4: Recovery Time

to outside help in the form of a good therapist or counselor. A good therapist or counselor will help you look at the situation from several perspectives; ask insightful questions to help you discover more effective alternatives; and offer analogies, metaphors, and stories from their experience, to help you see alternatives. All of these will help you become a more effective negotiator. For example, Cynthia says:

> My counselor always helped me come up with alternatives whenever I thought I only had one or two choices. By going into the negotiations with three or four alternatives that I thought were fair, I was able to assertively stand up for myself and I was seen as being more reasonable. My counselor also helped me see, that regardless of the financial settlement, the fact that I stood up for the principles that I believed in was the most important thing about our subsequent negotiations. It was important for me to hear this because left to my own devices, I may have given in and accepted or ruminated about the situation and stayed upset for a great deal more time than was necessary.

There are two types of difficult people that need special consideration: the alcoholic ex-spouse and the mentally ill ex-spouse.

After Leslie and Carl separated it became clear to Carl that Leslie had started drinking, at first only occasionally and then more frequently.

Exercise 28
Shortening Recovery Time

1. Give an example of how talking to someone who acted in the role of a recovery coach helped shorten your recovery time.

2. Effective negotiators have at least four people with whom they can talk, who are very effective in helping them learn from their mistakes and reduce their recovery time. In the space below, list four people you can turn to who can help you learn from your mistakes and reduce your recovery time:

   a. _____

   b. _____

   c. _____

   d. _____

I knew that there was a history of alcoholism in my ex-spouse's family, but Leslie had seemed to me to be your average social drinker from the time that I first met her until the time we separated 15 years later. During our marital breakdown she saw many marriage and individual counselors to no avail.

After we separated, I noticed the occasional slurred word and when I asked Leslie about this, she said it was the side effects from a new medication to help with her depression. However, as time when on, I noticed that she appeared to be drunk more and more frequently. I became really alarmed when she bashed in the front end of her car.

At this point I didn't know what to do. Confronting Leslie didn't work. She had become estranged from our friends and from her family, so I couldn't turn to them for help. I did not want to involve the children because this was an adult issue. I didn't know where to turn for help, when the counselor I was seeing suggested that I go to Drug Dependency and ask for help; there I found out that there was a vast array of options. Just knowing that there were so many options was a relief.

Among the options that my counselor listed were specific programs and interventions for the person who is alcohol or drug dependent such as Alcoholics Anonymous, Narcotics Anonymous, and/or by taking a drug called Antabuse, which when taken causes the person to become nauseated if he or she drinks alcohol. There is family therapy, which treats the whole family, and tribal therapy which treats the family, relatives, and friends. There are also different forms of help for the concerned significant other such as Al-Anon and Ala-Teen. If there are no Al-Anon meetings in your community, or if you are homebound, there are Al-Anon meetings available on the Internet and via telephone. Also, one book that my counselor recommended to me that was very helpful was *Get Your Loved One Sober: Alternatives to Nagging, Pleading, and Threatening* by Robert J. Myers (Hazelden, 2003).

* * *

My husband had always been a bit obsessive/compulsive when we were married, but he seemed to deteriorate after we separated. My children started complaining more and more about having to go over to Dad's. They told me that everything always had to be put back in its correct place and that Dad had really become a neatness freak. They complained that they never had any fun at his house and could they "please, please" stay at my house.

I tried to talk to Phillip about this but he usually got angry and said that I was to blame for being such a lax parent.

Because addictions and many mental health issues are not well understood by the general public and have a stigma attached to them, people are often in denial and don't seek help until they have hit rock bottom. Getting help from a qualified mental health professional can make all the difference between being a victim and a survivor, or a survivor and a thriver. It should be noted that there are a wide variety of different types of treatments and it is important to find the type of treatment and counselor that you would be comfortable with and who has the skills and training to help. All too often, getting separated or divorced shatters at least part of your support network and it is necessary to start rebuilding your support group sooner rather than later.

8. The Power of Building a Strong Support Network

The last topic we will cover in dealing with difficult people in your life is to eliminate them or deal with them as infrequently as possible and fill your life with people who are nurturing. Therefore, going through a separation and/or a divorce will mean that you have to develop, at least to a certain extent, a new support network.

Psychological research has shown that people with a strong support network cope more effectively with stress, including the stress of dealing with difficult people, in addition to living a longer life. However, at the same time that you are having to deal with the added stress of becoming or being divorced, your support system is also more likely not to work for you because many of the people who were in that support system will choose not to take sides and therefore will not be available for either of you. Some will take your side, while others will take your ex-spouse's side. In addition, most people who have not been separated or divorced will not realize that the stress of being separated and divorced does not dissipate in three months; it is in many ways much more like a death which may take up to two years or more to come to terms with. All of the research states that mourning, whether that be the death of a loved one or the loss of a relationship, takes hard work.

However, here again, there are noticeable differences between victims, survivors, and thrivers. Victims get depressed and stay depressed. They tend to play "poor me" and wear out their support networks. They tend to be totally reactive and do not or cannot take proactive steps to establish a new support network to help make up for the one they have lost. Survivors do the best job they can at dealing with and getting through their mourning. They are both reactive and proactive and usually rebuild a part of their support network. Thrivers actively mourn the relationship and dreams they have lost. However, at the appropriate time, they actively work to rebuild their support networks. They also realize that some of the people they come into contact with will be members of their support networks for a very short time and that this is how it should be. They also actively build a supportive and constructive support for the long-term.

Suzy's example follows.

> When my husband and I agreed to separate, one of my concerns was my own financial well-being and independence. So I went to my bank to secure my own line of credit and to develop a plan to pay off joint debts, including the mortgage. I met with and explained my new circumstances to Shelia, the bank's financial advisor, and explained my new circumstances. Shelia listened to me intently and with empathy and patience. Shelia then shared her own story which included a cheating husband, his pregnant lover, and the thousands of dollars spent on lawyer's fees in a bitter divorce.

> She talked about how women, at least economically, are still at the mercy of men in many ways even today, and the anger and frustration showed in her voice. With an evangelist's zeal, she vowed to help me in every way she could to secure lines of credit to the maximum as well as how to best leverage my assets. "OK, girl," she said as she sent my loan application online to be approved, "we are going to get you a whack of dough and then some." Shelia helped me immensely that day by normalizing my experience, helping me gain access to my own line of credit, and my newfound feelings of independence.

> I realized that as a separated woman, looking for financial independence, a pissed-off female loan manager is exactly who you want on your side.

Janet Conners is a very courageous woman and one of my personal heroes. Janet lost her husband, Randy, not to divorce but to AIDS. Randy was a hemophiliac and had become infected with HIV through tainted blood. This happened years ago and Janet subsequently became HIV positive. Janet then became the principal spokesperson for anyone who had HIV, regardless of how they got it. As an activist she wanted to put a heterosexual face on what had been perceived to be a gay man's and an intravenous drug user's disease. As a result of a great deal of media attention and the fact that Janet is such an eloquent spokesperson, she became very well known in every city and town across Canada.

When Janet's friends suggested that she go to a singles' dance, she laughed uproariously and said, "What are the chances that the most prominently known HIV-infected woman in Canada would even be asked to dance, let alone form a relationship?" The result was that on that night, she met Terry, an RCMP officer. They were subsequently married in June 2004.

Exercise 29
Rebuild Your Support Network

Please list three goals you can do to rebuild your own support network and next to each item, put the date by which you will have accomplished each goal.

Goal	Date by which the goal will be achieved
1	
2	
3	

Sometimes when we are seriously out of control and the usual remedies just don't seem to help, it's time to consider getting professional help. For example, I was in the midst of my divorce and leaving the marriage was not a problem for me; we had seriously tried to make it work, but it just wasn't workable. I was, however, having a very difficult time negotiating with my soon-to-be ex-spouse. What made matters worse was that I was teaching effective negotiating and influencing skills on an almost daily basis, and the principles and techniques that

I so eloquently taught just didn't seem to work that well with the one person in the world with whom I was having the most difficulty. A good friend of mine recommended that I see an excellent therapist. He was absolutely amazing and helped me get my life back in perspective. So if you are feeling overwhelmed and nothing you have done has helped, or if you are feeling overwhelmed by events outside, consider seeking professional help. But choose carefully, and don't let your pride get in the way.

9
Seek Mediation

During [mediation], an impartial professional ... helps divorcing couples to clearly define the issues in dispute and to reach agreements that are in the family's best interests.

— Alan L. Frankel, CSW

The biggest advantage of mediation is that it shelters and protects couples — and their children, if any — from the harmful effects of an adversarial divorce.

— Barbara Badolato, CSW, president of the
New York State Council on Divorce Mediation

Mediators come in all shapes and sizes and they have differing philosophies as to which are the best mediation practices and processes. If the parties were not able to resolve the dispute themselves, they could go to Aunt Hilda, a Priest, Minister, Rabbi, a financial advisor, or a professionally trained and/or certified mediator. The correct choice depends entirely on the parties involved in the mediation and the nature of the issues to be resolved. In some cases you may want to go with a court appointed mediator or you can hire a mediator who is in private practice.

Mediation is a form of assisted negotiation, and as such, it can be a very useful way to help parties who cannot reach agreement on their own to come to an agreement through the assistance of a qualified mediator. During the mediation process, the mediator's role is to be as neutral and as impartial as possible; however, mediators are not the decision-makers. Their role is to see if they can assist their clients arrive at a mutually acceptable resolution of the issues that brought them to mediation. One of the important tenets of mediation is that although we can't change or sometimes even agree on the past, we can have a positive impact on the future.

Since many people have no experience with mediation, it is not uncommon for the judicial system or family services to offer workshops to help people better understand the process of becoming separated and/or divorced and to better understand how mediation can be beneficial to the parents and children alike. For example, Eileen describes the workshop she attended on mediation prior to going to mediation with her ex-husband.

> I went to a three-hour workshop called "For the Sake of the Children," which explored the process of becoming separated and divorced, the impact on the parents, and how to minimize adverse affects on children. What a surreal but helpful experience. We spent a lot of time on Kubler-Ross's stages in death and dying and how the stages applied to going through a divorce. Then they showed a video titled "The Experts on Divorce — Kids." The film showed a half hour with children talking about what they need in the situation and their advice to parents who are separating. The film was heartwrenching, powerful, and helpful.

> They also covered the legal aspects of separation and talked about the various types of separation that a relationship goes through: emotional, physical, economic, etc. I also learned about another kind of counselor at this workshop. Instead of marriage counselors, there are separation counselors.

I followed up with Eileen after she completed the sessions with her separation counselor. She described what she got out of the sessions as follows.

> I was both fascinated and horrified in the meetings with the separation counselor. The two most important things I learned were that I will never really understand my ex-husband and how he thinks and this has helped to confirm that we made the right decision to end our marriage. I also

> have more faith that we can continue to be excellent parents and have a decent, business-like relationship.

Sometimes if one of the ex-spouses wants to go to mediation and the other one does not, an introductory workshop can provide solid information on which to base a decision about going to mediation or not. Likewise, many people who were at first reluctant to go felt that they could make a better decision after having a one-on-one interview with a skilled mediator about how the mediation process works. This can be especially helpful when one of the ex-spouses is pushing for mediation, because that person is often the last person that the other ex-spouse wants to be influenced by. It also helps if the parties know that mediation works in helping people reach an agreement, or at least a partial agreement, approximately 80 percent of the time. Last, mediation does not preclude other forms of dispute resolution, if the mediation does not work. The parties still have the option of negotiating through their lawyers and/or of going to court.

An in-depth example of how a mediator used a framing statement, helped a divorcing couple identify interests, and creatively used objective criteria to help each party maximize their interests in a way that they may never have thought of on their own, is used to illustrate how these concepts were applied.

1. The Importance of a Framing Statement

A framing statement is like a mission statement for a business or volunteer organization. Only in this case, the framing statement is about developing the best process possible to help all of the parties involved move forward. An excellent framing statement helps set the tone of the meeting and identifies the overriding goal(s) for the process by answering the question as to why the parties have come to seek mediation and what they hope to achieve from the process. The framing statement may come at any point in the mediation, but often is developed near the beginning of the session and is, for all intents and purposes, a mission statement as to how the process of mediation can help the parties benefit from mediation. It is important to note that the framing statement can be modified and improved upon at any point in the mediation.

The framing statement must be as inclusive and neutral as possible in representing all of the parties' overriding interests. Developing a good framing statement is much like adding salt to the soup. It depends on the tastes of the individuals involved, but you know when you have it right. An example of a framing statement the mediator developed with the couple in our example who were in the process of separating and divorcing follows:

Sample 7
Framing Statement

We are here today to see if we can develop options that will help you maximize your assets and minimize the costs associated with your divorce. At the same time, we will work on developing a shared parenting agreement that is fair and equitable as possible for both the parents and the children.

Once the framing statement has been formulated, it is time to identify each party's interests.

2. The Importance of Identifying both Parties' Underlying Interests

The mediator worked with this couple to identify, as closely as possible, their underlying interests. The reader will note that many of the couple's interests are shared. What makes negotiation possible is that when asked to rank their interests in order of importance, they assigned differing priorities to their interests, (as the numbers in parenthesis after each interest indicates). The interests of both the husband and wife, as well as the ranking of each of their interest, can be found in Table 4.

From the analysis in Table 4, it is readily apparent how many of this couple's interests were shared interests. Without putting all of their interests on paper, it would have been next to impossible for them to see how many shared interests they actually had. In addition, putting their interests on paper helped this couple to focus on the problem rather than on each other, in other words, to separate the people from the problem. An impartial third-party mediator made it much easier for this couple to follow this process than would have been the case if they tried to proceed on their own. In other words, both the objective criteria and an impartial mediator helped the parties move away from positional bargaining and use more objective problem solving.

Table 4
Parties' Interests

Husband's Interests	Wife's Interests:
To be and to feel to be treated fairly (1)	To be and to feel to be treated fairly (1)
To be able to retire comfortably (3)	To be able to retire comfortably (6)
Buy a house or set of flats with maximum down payment and minimum mortgage (6)	Buy a house or set of flats with maximum down payment and minimum mortgage (3)
Have our children's future education provided for (5)	Have our children's future education provided for (5)
Have our age difference and the amount of capital I brought into the marriage recognized in a manner that is fair (4)	Feel that our 11.5 year marriage is fairly recognized in the settlement (4)
To be able to keep my inheritance which would keep intact a bond between me and my parents (6)	
Settle these issues as quickly as possible so we can both get on with our lives with a maximum of autonomy and to be able to co-parent our children as effectively as possible (2)	Settle these issues as quickly as possible so we can both get on with our lives with a maximum of autonomy and to be able to co-parent our children as effectively as possible (2)
Both parties will have a reliable car (8)	Both parties will have a reliable car (7)
Furniture will be divided equally, both parties will retain the furniture they owned before the marriage (9)	Furniture will be divided equally, both parties will retain the furniture they owned before the marriage (8)

3. The Creative Use of Objective Criteria

Thomas F. Crum said, "Resolving conflict is rarely about who is right. It is about acknowledgment and appreciation of differences." Objective criteria can be one of your best friends as a negotiator when it helps prevent all of the parties from being positional or reaching agreements based on power and subsequent retribution which leads to agreements that are not carried out and damages relationships which in turn poisons future negotiations.

There are also many situations where there are multiple objective criteria to choose from and it is not uncommon for the parties to become positional about whose objective criteria are the most fair and reasonable. There are other situations where objective criteria just do not seem to exist. Under these types of circumstances, one needs to be as innovative and creative as possible in developing criteria and then select the most fair and objective criteria possible. In this case, you will be able to see how the creation of objective criteria helped this couple come to as amicable an agreement as possible.

According to this couple's local divorce laws, all of the assets from the marriage would be divided equally between the separating spouses, as this couple had been married for more than 10 years. The husband in this case was 11 years older than the wife and had considerably more assets than she did coming into the marriage. Clearly, he would have felt that such a settlement was terribly unfair.

However, the wife had sacrificed many years of her career, in which she devoted, either on a full-time or on a part-time basis, to childrearing. As well, the children deserved to have a comparable lifestyle in each of the new households. If one parent were substantially better off than the other, this would violate the interest of fair and equitable treatment of the children.

The mediator helped this couple fashion a much better solution than the one-size-fits-all solution that they might have used if they strictly followed their state or provincial guidelines. The development of objective criteria was key to finding a solution that both parties could live with.

In this case the husband, who at 52, was 11 years older than the wife, who was 41. Both individuals were professionally employed and most of their retirement funds were in 401Ks. To be more precise, the husband had approximately $250,000 invested in his retirement savings account and the wife had approximately $125,000 in her 401K. Using the Divorce Act, as one set of objective criteria, these two amounts would be added and subsequently divided by two, which would result in $187,500 each for the husband and for the wife.

A different set of objective criteria would be to estimate the amount both the husband and wife would need to retire comfortably if they each kept their respective 401Ks. They consulted a financial planner who suggested that the couple could use age 65, the traditional age of retirement, as one possible guideline. Then estimating that the wife would live approximately five years longer than the husband, and being conservative on the rate of return on their investments, the financial planner estimated the value of their respective retirement saving plans upon their subsequent retirements. The results of this analysis demonstrated that although the two amounts, $250,000 and $125,000, look substantially different in today's dollars, allowing for the fact that the wife's estimated date of retirement (assuming she retires at age 65) is 13 years later than the husband's (assuming that he also retires at age 65), the wife's estimated number of years left to contribute to her 401K is 24 years. In this case, the best estimation is that this couple's 401Ks at the time of their respective retirements would be equal. It also had to be taken into consideration that there is some uncertainty built into this estimate because no one knows how their 401Ks will be valued at the time of their respective retirements. This risk factor also needed to be accounted for in their settlement.

Combining the above information with the fact that the wife valued liquidity (that is, having enough money to buy a house mortgage free) to a much greater degree than the husband, this couple was able to work out an agreement based on their interests that was substantially more satisfying to them than the one size fits all solution which consisted of simply dividing all of the assets equally. In this case, the couple decided that the husband could keep all of the money he had acquired in his 401Ks, which helped him prepare for his retirement. The wife, who valued having a house that was mortgage-free, received enough money to buy her house without having to take out a mortgage, while the husband did have to obtain a mortgage. The settlement appealed to both parties because the husband valued his retirement over being mortgage-free, while the wife valued being mortgage-free over her retirement as she had more years in which she could work and add to her 401K.

Could this couple have come to such an amicable agreement if they didn't explore various objective criteria? I think not. Developing multiple criteria helped them look at their problem from multiple viewpoints. Looking at their problem from multiple viewpoints helped them develop multiple options. I asked this couple if they could have arrived at this solution without the aid of a mediator and without using multiple objective criteria. They emphatically said no. I asked them to further explain how a mediator helped them come to an amicable solution. They said that at the time, even though they both knew they had to separate and had truly tried to make their marriage work, the process was unbearably painful, and it was much easier to talk to each other through an objective, impartial mediator.

I asked them how they chose Denise as their mediator; they said that Denise was the financial advisor that they both had been using for the previous 12 years. Both parties said they respected their accountant, he knew their financial situation well, and he also had a great deal of experience helping other divorcing couples divide their marital assets. Their financial advisor, like all good mediators, helped the couple to agree on ground rules before they began the mediation process. Among the ground rules were: full disclosure, fairness, the use of objective criteria, and focusing on mutual gains to the greatest degree possible. The outcome for this couple was as fair as possible under the circumstances and each ex-spouse said that their final agreement worked out much better for them than a traditional one-size-fits-all agreement.

4. What to Look for in Selecting a Mediator

Although mediation is a fairly recent development in conflict resolution, it is becoming an increasingly widespread and popular alternative to the traditionally more adversarial practices. The fact that it is becoming more widespread and popular can be a double-edged sword. There are now a large number of mediators. In some cases, these practitioners are certified and in some cases they are not. You should choose your mediator with the same care that you would choose your physician, lawyer or financial advisor; the stakes are high and the outcomes can potentially last a lifetime.

How do you find a good mediator? Word-of-mouth is one good place to start. It takes a long time to develop an excellent reputation, so take full advantage of that fact. Family, friends, acquaintances, or other professionals can be an excellent place to start. Since mediation is a relatively new option, there may be less knowledge publicly available to you than you would have access to in, for example, finding a family physician. Also, some people view it as a failure if they can't work out their differences and therefore may be less willing to share information about the mediation process or even the fact that they saw a mediator. In sum, make sure that any potential mediator has a good, solid reputation and think about obtaining several endorsements. You can also interview the person on the phone or in person.

Don't be afraid to change mediators if you feel that the person is not doing a good job or is showing bias. As a professional courtesy, tell the mediator your concerns. If you can clear up a minor misunderstanding, you may save a lot of time and money, rather than having to start over again with a new mediator.

If you or your ex-spouse are hesitant to try mediation, an excellent way to give mediation a fair chance is to go to one session and then base your willingness to continue on the reality of how helpful having a neutral third party was to your ongoing discussions with your ex-spouse. Just like you would not take out your own appendix, it is sometimes equally difficult to try to negotiate a conflict if you are one of the parties in that conflict. To help you find a mediator, there are state, provincial and national family mediation association practitioner lists, and there are public legal information services that can help you find a qualified mediator. Many family courts are now offering mediation services or referrals to qualified mediators.

5. How the Mediation Process Works

Typically the mediator helps the participants tell their stories, identify their interests, and then draft creative solutions to maximize each party's interests. The mediator then looks at how to develop an implementation plan, asks the participants to have the plan verified by their lawyers, and looks at developing a process whereby the parties can receive additional help if they have difficulties in the future.

Most mediators try and get a sense of the issues involved in the dispute, e.g., co-parenting arrangements, discipline, communication, property settlements, etc. No two disputes are alike. As the mediator interviews participants they get a sense of how many issues there are to resolve. The higher the number of issues, the longer it may take to find a resolution. There are typically varying interests underneath each issue.

A mediator should be knowledgeable about the mediation process and skillful in applying the skills that are used in that process. Among the skills that an effective mediator should have developed to a high degree are objectivity, active listening, questioning, reframing, and the ability to help turn negatives into positives. The mediator will also help his or her clients shift from blaming to taking joint responsibility for finding creative solutions to help in resolving the issues that brought them to mediation in the first place. In addition, the couples who come to mediation also learn a method and valuable skills that can help them solve new issues that will arise in the future.

Mediators can frequently facilitate a conversation between a couple that the couple may not be able to have on their own. When couples try conversations on their own, emotions often run high and participants get stuck saying the same things over and over. The mediation process slows down the conversation, and focuses on mutual understanding and respectful expression of emotion.

Mediators also tend to focus on better ways to create a mutually satisfactory future. The mediator can help the participants express their grief, sadness, and/or unhappiness about the past, and at the same time help their clients realize that although they cannot change the past, they can create a different and more mutually satisfying future. Although mediation tends to be focused on the future, there are times when the mediator can help clear up misunderstandings from the past and/or develop a better understanding of why each party behaved as they did. It is also important to realize that all mediators do not use the same approach and have developed their own style of mediation. For example, some mediators will not suggest options that may allow the parties to reach agreement; rather, they assist the parties in developing their own options. Other mediators are more interventionist and will suggest options, although the mediator(s) should always suggest more than one option to avoid suggesting an option that favors, or appears to favor one person or the other. Therefore, it is up to the clients to make sure that they are comfortable with the style of the mediator they select.

Mediation will help the parties tell their stories. By listening to these stories the mediators will also help the parties listen to each other. This is important because feeling understood is one of the basic human needs. By feeling understood, the parties are often more willing to let go of the past, which is one of the first steps they need to take in order to create a better future.

Mediation will also help the parties articulate what they need in language that is as neutral as possible. The sentence begins with "what I need." For example, "I need you to understand that I feel that the children are angry," or "I need you to ask questions about the children based on your observations and interactions with them." Mediation can help both parties identify what they need to get to move forward in the separated/divorced world in which they find themselves living. Mediation also focuses on helping the parties speak for themselves, and not make judgments about the other person's intentions.

Sometimes, there are issues and values that cannot be mediated and the ex-spouses are not going to be able to agree on some issues such as: "How clean is clean?" or "When should the children be disciplined and how quickly and how severe should the consequences be if the child misbehaves?" These are fundamental values, and sometimes the mediator's job is to help their clients learn how to agree to disagree and not allow those value differences to poison the relationship between the ex-spouses or between the ex-spouses and their children.

For example, one issue that frequently comes up are differences of opinion over when to discipline, how often to discipline, and how much to discipline. Or how similar or different can your styles of discipline be without negatively affecting the children. Or, how much will discipline be shared or not shared with the other parent. Therefore, it is often very helpful if the ex-spouses can develop and/or be helped to develop a joint definition of cooperative parenting. An example of a co-parenting agreement from one of the people I interviewed for this book appears in Sample 2 in Chapter 4 and also on the download kit that came with this book.

What happens if you want to write a co-parenting agreement and your ex-spouse refuses? My sense is that this is still a good exercise to try to write one, as it provides you with a statement of your clear intentions and writing that statement will help you behave in a manner that is more aligned with those intentions. Second, although your ex-spouse may not engage in the written exercise, he or she may decide to act in a similar manner, and/or he or she may agree to develop a co-parenting agreement at a later time. In summary, there are benefits to writing a co-parenting agreement for yourself regardless of what your ex-spouse chooses to do. However, given the state of the relationship between the two "heads of state," it could be wise to share the agreement with your ex-spouse, or it could be wise to keep it as a private document for your use only.

You can also agree to disagree on small issues where a court wouldn't adjudicate on those issues. Examples of some of the issues that a court would typically not tend to see are questions about whether a child should play a particular sport, quarrels over pick-up time, how healthy different types of food are, or differences in opinion on allowance.

Sometimes you can resolve some parts of an issue, but not others. For example, you have an agreement on how to share the Christmas holidays, doctor's appointments, activities at school, and birthdays, but not custody, so you would send custody back to the courts. A very important use of mediation is a process of identifying the issues about which the couple wants to reach agreement, which ones they can reach agreement on, and which ones they can't. Mediation can help the disputants narrow the issues that eventually need to go to litigation.

Mediation can also help the parties develop a process for resolving current and future conflicts. In other cases the parties may be able to apply what they have learned through the mediation process and/or modify a creative solution from a past mediation to resolve current and future problems and/or develop guidelines for when they should return to mediation.

6. Ground Rules and Guidelines

One of the first tasks of the mediation process is the establishment of ground rules and guidelines. Among the ground rules that are most helpful are no personal attacks, respectful listening, no interruptions (part of no interruptions is that the parties can write down points and counterpoints they would like to state and that person will get a fair hearing), and an agreement to disclose relevant information. Appropriate disclosure is an important part of the agreement to mediate and is often essential to successful mediation. Parties cannot make good, lasting decisions without the appropriate information.

For example, if a divorced or separated couple has an agreement that their children sleep at one parent's house three nights a week but the other parent don't know that his or her ex-spouse has a new partner who is also sleeping there, when the other parent finds out from the children, it may ignite a new conflict or rekindle an old one. Therefore, having an agreement on what information is appropriate to disclose and what types of information best remain private can be a very valuable part of the mediation process. In addition, there is often a ground rule in mediation on speaking for oneself rather than impugning the motives of the other party.

Once the ground rules and guidelines are established, the mediator or mediators can then gently remind the participants when the guidelines are not being followed. In addition, it is not uncommon in the first session, depending on the level of anger, for a mediator to ask the participants to speak directly to the mediator rather than to each other. Other guidelines that may be agreed to are that either party and/or the mediators can break off the mediation if no progress is being made. Also, if the parties are able to resolve most but not all of the issues, they can sign off on the ones they agreed to and go to court to resolve the outstanding issues, or they can take all of the matters to court. Even if going to court is the final outcome, often the mediation process has helped the parties to clarify their thinking which can make the court proceedings more efficient. There is one other issue that is often covered in the ground rules, and that is caucusing.

6.1 Caucusing

It is sometimes very difficult for a divorcing couple or ex-spouses to trust each other or even to talk to each other. Feelings are strong, both sides feel justified, both parties may feel that they have lost either financially, or in terms of a sense of family and/or self-esteem. Also, due to past difficulties, the parties may be unwilling or unable to communicate with each other. Each party may be afraid of losing face if he or she is the first one to make a concession. In cases like these, caucusing may prove to be very effective. Caucusing involves the mediator meeting with individual parties privately.

The ground rules for caucusing are usually determined early in the mediation process. The most commonly used rule for caucusing are that the mediator(s) and/or each participant can ask for a private meeting with the mediator or mediators at any time in the mediation process. All discussions within the caucus are confidential unless permission is given to share some or all of the content with the other party in the mediation.

During the caucus it is possible to further explore the party's interests, to examine different types of objective criteria and develop creative solutions, and/or explore possible trade-offs. Among the reasons caucusing works so well is that there is no history between the mediator and the disputants. The disputants tend to be more free from any emotional history when the other disputant leaves the room. As well, trained mediators are respectful listeners, and they can pose questions that can help the disputants think more clearly and creatively. As the relationship that brings the disputants to mediation is likely to be quite stressful, and stress is the enemy of creativity, the discussions between each of the disputants and the mediator(s) fosters conditions for a freer, more wide-ranging and a more creative problem-solving process.

After the mediator(s) has/have caucused with both parties the mediation resumes again, the process of caucusing often bringing the parties closer to agreement, and/or developing a mutually agreed-upon process that will bring them to agreement eventually.

It is also sometimes helpful, if there is more than one mediator, for the mediators to caucus among themselves to discuss various aspects of the mediation and brainstorm options in order to ensure that they are providing the best process possible, to calibrate their perceptions, and/or to discuss possible strategies to improve the process. The mediators may also need to discuss whether a break is needed or if the mediation should continue or be terminated. The mediators will also need to decide which aspects of their discussion should be made public to the participants and which aspects should remain private between the mediators.

6.2 Defining the role of the mediator

Another method mediators can use to obtain input from the participants is to ask them to help define the role of the mediator. By asking them for their input, the mediator can find out at least part of their expectations. Where the party's expectations differ from those of the mediator, the role of the mediator can be negotiated between the parties. After being successful in this negotiation, the parties will have more confidence that they can negotiate the more controversial issues that have brought them to mediation.

One of the things that mediation expert Lawrence Susskind does, which demonstrates his openness, is to tell the participants that if they ever find that he is not being impartial, to tell him up front. If they find that he is being partial to the point that it affects the process, they can fire him and either find a new mediator or he will help them find a new mediator. Being this open helps the participants in the mediation be more open.

I usually use an analogy to help the participants understand the length of time that mediation takes. Without doing this, the participants are often too impatient with the process because they do not understand the process. The analogy is about rescuing 18-month-old Baby Jessica who had fallen into a well. The rescuers had to work as quickly as possible to get her out of the well. At the same time they had to be careful about not working so quickly that they caused the well to cave in. It is much the same with mediation; sometimes we have to go slow to go fast.

You may be asked to sign an agreement to be in mediation. Often, part of the agreement is that the proceedings of the mediation are not to be used against each other if the issues proceed to court. In legal terms, one could say that the mediation proceedings are done without prejudice. In other words, confidentiality helps people to be honest and to come up with interesting solutions without feeling that they will be held to them in another forum.

Lastly, one of the most important roles the mediator can play is to help the parties clarify the issues in a neutral enough manner that they can be resolved as fairly as possible. By talking about what is as fair as possible, it helps the participants realize that they may never get an agreement that each party thinks is completely fair. However, if both parties can live with the agreement, and/or if they think it is equally unfair, they are much more likely to accept the real life limitations as to what is fair and then be able to move on with their lives.

6.3 Brainstorming

At some point, the mediators will introduce the idea of brainstorming. To set the stage for brainstorming out-of-the-box solutions, the mediators may ask the participants to give examples of creative solutions that they have used to resolve problems in the past. Part of the guidelines for brainstorming is that no criticism of any kind is allowed during the brainstorming process.

6.4 Transaction costs

It is not uncommon for the parties to be closer to a resolution than they thought they were. The mediators can help both parties see how far apart they are and also look at the transaction costs of not reaching an agreement.

For example, we had some new carpeting installed on our staircase and throughout the upstairs hallway of our house. During the installation process one of the ceramic tiles in the bathroom was accidentally cracked. Although the tiles were still in very good condition, it was no longer possible to find a suitable tile to replace the cracked tile. Since the crack was near the door, the contractor and I agreed to use a wider molding which would cover the crack. However, the molding extended too far into the bathroom. One possible solution was to replace the whole floor at a cost of $582.50. The contractor offered $75. I countered with half of the cost of the floor at $291.25. He countered at 25 percent of the cost of a new floor at $145.66, at which point there seemed to be no further movement. We were exactly $145.66 apart. One solution was to go to small claims court. The question the mediators asked was, "Is it worth our time and effort to go to court for $145.66 where a judge would decide the amount owing and we would have less control over the final outcome?" The answer was clearly no, as the parties were relatively close and neither party wanted to continue the conflict. The transaction costs were prohibitive. On the other hand, neither party could agree to move from their 50 percent and 25 percent compensation proposal.

However, during the brainstorming session, a creative proposal emerged that was acceptable to both parties. The solution was as follows. The bill would be reduced by 50 percent of the replacement value of the flooring. Therefore, I could claim that I was true to my beliefs. At the same time, the plaintiff would receive half of the amount owing and the other half would be donated to charity. The brainstormed solution allowed both parties to feel that they were treated as fairly as possible. It was a win for both parties and a win for a charity.

One couple were at complete loggerheads as to when their 13-year-old daughter Kelly should start dating. Mary, Kelly's mother, felt that Kelly was very mature for her age and could start dating now. George, Kelly's father, was of the exact opposite opinion. An example of a framing statement regarding the appropriate age at which George and Mary's daughter Kelly could start dating was:

> By agreeing on the same rules and guidelines it will make it easier for both of us to parent and at the same time we want to avoid setting a precedent where Kelly is able to play one parent off against the other. Let's see if we can develop some graduated dating guidelines that will work for all three of us.

When they brainstormed creative options, they agreed that Kelly could go out on group dates for the time being. They agreed that her parents would know who was involved in the group dates and they agreed on the fact that Kelly had to be home at 10:00 p.m. unless both parents agreed to any exceptions. They also all agreed that this policy would be in effect for six months and that all of the parties would meet when the six months were up and decide at that time if any changes in the agreement should be made.

One example where the transaction costs appear to have been way too high is the parents who had gone to court over which school their child should attend. No matter which school the child ends up at, the parents may have provided their daughter with the worst education possible and that is the importance of how to get along and resolve problems constructively rather than destructively. Another case is that of a 14-year-old boy who had lost 11 pounds in a hunger strike over his parents' custody battle. In this case, the boy was attempting to get the courts to let him live with his father, although legal custody was his mother's.

What percentage of family mediations are successful? It is difficult to say because there are no agreed-upon definitions of success. However, the few studies that have been done estimate that the percentage of successful mediations is 80 percent.

7. Memorandums of Understanding

If it is not in writing, it doesn't exist.

Mediators will often help the parties develop Memorandums of Understanding (MOU). Every issue is different, but agreeing on the underlying principles to help resolve an issue can also be helpful in helping the parties see that issues can be resolved and in providing a model to help resolve other and/or new issues that will invariably come up. Every MOU is different and if they agree, they agree because they have moved to something creative; that's what collaborative problem solving is about. Among the issues that a MOU that separating and divorcing couples might cover are:

- Decision-making.
- Primary residence.
- Scheduling of holidays and vacations.
- Relations with new partners.
- One parent wanting to move for career and/or other reasons.
- Helping the children develop good relationships with both parents.

Often having the MOU written can avoid confusions over who agreed to what and it also helps to make sure that the language is as clear as possible. Philosopher Bertrand Russell said that most disputes could be reduced to a single paragraph if all of the terms were adequately defined. Therefore, most mediators will also look at an agreement and ensure that the MOU passes the SWAB test, where S stands for specific, W stands for written, A stands for attainable, and B stands for balanced. If an agreement does not pass the SWAB test, it will probably not stand the test of time. Last, MOUs often have a clause suggesting what the parties can do if the MOU becomes unworkable, or needs to be changed because of new and/or unforeseen circumstances. Often this clause will have an invitation to return to mediation should it prove necessary.

8. Finding Mediators in Unlikely Places

When my ex-wife and I separated, some issues such as sorting out the furniture were relatively easy and painless. Other issues, like dividing our financial assets, were anything but easy and painless. Enter Dennis, the person who we both used as our accountant. Dennis offered to mediate. He had done this for various clients over the years and he was a logical choice for us. First, he knew our individual and joint financial situations and we had both built up a high degree of comfort and trust in Dennis over the years. Second, he knew the tax laws and could help us work out the most favorable settlement possible. Third, we trusted Dennis to be fair, neutral, and impartial, and he was.

When we met with Dennis, he had only one rule for the mediation and that was complete and full financial disclosure. If we agreed, we could go forward. If not, the mediation was off. Dennis then helped us work out as fair an agreement as possible. It is also accurate to say that, although each of us thought that we deserved more at the time, in retrospect the mediation process was a starting point in helping each of us rebuild our financial lives, which would also help us start to rebuild our personal lives. There are several sources that can be of help when trying to resolve financial issues. Among those sources of help are: financial counselors, financial advisors, accountants, and written material that can help the ex-spouses look at their financial situations more objectively and help them retain as much of their income and investments as possible.

Exercise 30
Financial Help

If you are dealing with the financial aspects of separating and/or divorcing, or if there are financial issues that came up after the divorce, and you need help in resolving them, who could you turn to for help? Make a list.

For financial assistance, you may have benefits through your EAP (Employee Assistance Program) or third party insurance. EAP is a program that many employers offer their employees and different programs offer a differing degree of services. As well, many employees have benefits such as dental, physiotherapy and counseling. Some EAPs and benefit programs cover mediation while others do not.

Linda had separated from her husband three years ago. She had two major problems. First, her ex-husband, Phil, was no longer spending very much time with their daughter Tiffany, who was feeling hurt and rejected. Recently Phil had started a relationship with another woman who had two children. His infrequent visits with Tiffany became events where he dragged her around with his new girlfriend and her children. He would leave the children to their own devices while he and his girlfriend did adult things around the house. Every time Linda tried to talk to Phil, he would verbally agree to spend more one-on-one time with Tiffany. Linda made it clear she understood he had a new relationship but asked that he carve out some time for Tiffany where it was just the two of them during their visits. He would agree, but his promises seldom turned into reality.

On one occasion Linda tried to speak to Phil about her parenting concerns when he was dropping Tiffany off after a visit. He had once again brought her back over an hour late. Linda was very irritated about that before he got there. When they started to talk their conversation turned into a negatively spiraling ping-pong match of accusations and counter-accusations, which ended with Linda accusing Phil of not being responsible, and Phil accusing Linda of being a "control freak."

After the confrontation, Linda decided that this must stop and she would work to build a better working relationship with Phil and see if she could convince Phil to spend more quality one-on-one time with Tiffany.

Linda reviewed her benefits at work and found out that she and Phil had access to a mediator through her EAP. She convinced Phil to try one session to see if they could improve their joint parenting. The session went well as did the two subsequent sessions. The other part of Linda's plan was to negotiate with Phil primarily through email. Linda stated that "using email allows me to more carefully select my words and my tone." Linda added that, "the other advantage of using email was that some of the non-verbal behavior that I am sure bugged each of us both during our marriage and after was no longer present, and thusly, the likelihood of escalating our conflicts was much less likely to happen." In addition, there was a written record so they did not have to rely on memory. As a result they have a much better co-parenting relationship and Tiffany now feels that she has a father again. Linda's last comment was that she doubted if she and Phil would have been able to make these changes on their own. The mediation followed by the email method of communicating made all of the difference in the world.

Exercise 31 will help you more fully appreciate the power of using objective criteria in the negotiating process.

Exercise 31
Thinking about Mediation

Can you think of a situation where the addition of a formal or informal mediator or mediators helped the parties resolve a conflict or a dispute? Write it down.

Are you currently involved in a negotiation, conflict or dispute wherein the addition of a mediator or mediators could aid in themsettlement of the problem? If so, what are some suggestions for finding a mediator?

If the ex-spouses are too angry, too emotionally hooked, or to adversarial to try mediation, or if the mediation does not work, or if the ex-spouses can resolve some of the issues and not others, they can try a cooling off period and/or try seeing another mediator who may be able to help them. Alternatively, it may be time to consult a lawyer or lawyers. One word of caution: Hire your lawyer with the same care that you would select a surgeon. It is for this reason that more information on working with or through lawyers follows.

9. Negotiating through Lawyers

Surgeons operate on your body. Divorce lawyers operate on your family. Therefore you want to hire your divorce lawyer with the same care that you would hire a surgeon. One way to be proactive is to make sure that you both use lawyers who use a cooperative approach and have a history of being able to work together. There have been horror stories of couples who have worked out a fair and reasonable agreement only to have their lawyers turn it into a fight. Another crucial fact to remember is that your lawyer works for you and should give you advice but it is you who makes the final decisions. Therefore, it is always helpful to know your end objectives when you consult a lawyer.

9.1 When to hire a cooperative lawyer

If both parties sincerely want to cooperate and want to be as fair and honest as possible, they should definitely hire lawyers who have a reputation for being fair and for being able to work together cooperatively. The result is that the proceedings will then be more amicable, less aggressive, take less time, and cost less money. The agreements will be more creative and do a better job of satisfying all of the parties' interests including: ex-spouses', children's, and relatives'. These proceedings will also go a long way in laying the foundation for your future interactions and may be models that you can follow in forming future agreements. An ideal strategy, as previously stated, is for the parties to select lawyers who know and respect each other and have a reputation for being able to work cooperatively, both with their clients and with each other. These are questions that can be asked in advance when you select your lawyers. For example, Pat conducted in-depth interviews with six lawyers before making her final choice and reported that the time spent finding the right lawyer was definitely worth the effort.

> I found the most amazing lawyer who specializes in "family-friendly divorces." He focuses on helping families maximize their resources by coming up with a creative separation and co-parenting agreement. He then sends one spouse to another lawyer at the end of the process to make sure all parties' interests are covered.

When one lawyer turns out to be too aggressive, the party who hired that lawyer should consider changing lawyers, as Cory's story points out.

> My ex-wife Josephine's lawyer was very confrontational and aggressive. He was the kind of guy who, when he played sports, had to win. He was very combative and turned it into a turf war. For him, it was a game, winning was the only option, and it didn't matter who the casualties were, including our children. He really had it in for me and for my lawyer as well.
>
> Eventually he went so far that my ex-wife and her parents decided that it couldn't continue. She hired a much more cooperative lawyer and although the negotiations had their difficult issues to negotiate, we achieved a settlement that we all felt was fairly reasonable and her changing lawyers did a lot to repair the damage to our relationship that her first lawyer caused.

One of the most important things that we can learn from Cory and Josephine's experience is that the ex-spouses who have had children together will have to get along for many years after the divorce. In fact, the divorce settlement and to a certain extent the separation agreement are the foundation on which their future relationship will be built. You will have to live on top of that foundation for a much longer period of time than the lawyers will, so choose your lawyers carefully.

If the other party won't change lawyers, then you have an interesting choice to make. You can see if your lawyer is strong enough to stand up to the aggressive lawyer or you may need to find a more aggressive lawyer. There is an interesting law firm that has a two-pronged approach. Their clients usually start with a cooperative lawyer. If the other side does not reciprocate, they send in their most aggressive lawyer.

9.2 When to hire an aggressive lawyer

Consider hiring an aggressive lawyer when your ex-spouse or his or her lawyer is malicious. For example, Daniel states:

> My ex-wife was using every dirty trick in the book in order to get sole custody of the children, limit my access to my children, and have me pay through the nose. First, she accused me of beating her and was able to secure a restraining order that prevented me from seeing my children, even though there was no evidence that supported her accusations. My lawyer said to be patient as we would counter her claims when we went to court. This was absolutely unacceptable to me so I hired a more aggressive lawyer. He suggested that we do two things. First, we would move to get the restraining order removed and second, we would have the children assessed by a clinical psychologist. Although this would add greatly to my expenses, I felt that I had to act fast to prove I was not an abusive husband and protect my rights as a father. In the end, the judge believed that I was not abusive and my ex-wife's strategy worked against her rather than for her.

9.3 Going to court

Be careful about exaggerating the truth because often a judge will see through it and instead of helping you get what you want, you will often get less of what you want, as the following example points out.

Gary and Estelle were married for three years and had a son named Zack. Estelle felt that she was too young to be tied down to family life and left two-year-old Zack in the care of his father when she moved from Thunder Bay to Toronto. Estelle kept in contact with Zack and saw him at twice a year, at Christmas and during the summer.

When Zack turned 16, Estelle tried to regain custody of him. By this time she was making a significantly higher income than Gary and tried to bribe Zack with all of the newest material objects that any boy could want. She also told him that his father had had his turn and now it was her turn to have Zack live with her.

The judge asked Estelle how she thought Zack would feel about leaving his father, his high school friends, and the type of social support that Zack would have in Toronto. Estelle said she didn't think that would be a problem. The judge asked her if she talked to Zack about this and she said no. Estelle then added that she made at least twice as much as Zack's father.

In the end, the judge ruled that Zack should stay with his father, but since Estelle was now making more money, the judge would increase the amount of child support that Estelle had to pay Gary.

10. Parallel Parenting

In another case, a person I interviewed for the book said she was in a five-year custody battle with her ex-husband. The battle took place in three states and the disputants used a total of six lawyers. At one time they lived across the street from each other. In cases like this, it might be better to consider parallel parenting, which was developed specifically for those couple who will never be able to get along.

Dr. Philip M. Stahl published a book titled *Parenting After Divorce* (Impact Publishers, 2007), where he outlines the benefits of parallel parenting. The main benefit of parallel parenting is that it helps the parents disengage from their conflict with each other so that they can parent as effectively as possible, and the children will not feel caught between their parents. The basic rule of parallel parenting is that each parent parents the child his or her way when the child is staying with each him or her, in essence, establishing a "demilitarized zone" around the children. Stahl states that among the indications that parallel parenting may be necessary are:

- Continuation of hostility that began during the marriage.

- Differing perceptions of pre-separation child-rearing roles.

- Differing perceptions of post-separation child-rearing roles.

- Differing perceptions of how to parent.

- Concern about the adequacy of the other parent's parenting ability.

- An unwillingness of one or both parents to accept the end of the relationship.

- Jealousy about a new partner in the other parent's life.

- Contested child custody issues.

- Personality factors in one or both parents that stimulate conflict.

Examples of specific issues that will be decided jointly are related to health, education, religion, and other areas that are considered important information. Perhaps the best way to gain an understating of how parallel parenting works is through Stahl's own words: "Important information means the health, welfare, and interests of your child. If your child is sick, you will inform the other parent of this fact, with details on what medication is needed, what has already been administered, and when the next dose is to be given. If your child has a school field trip, you will inform the other parent of the details, and use your parenting plan to decide who might go with the child on the field trip. Each of you should develop independent relationships with your child's teachers, doctors, coaches, and friends so that you don't have to rely on the other parent for your information. Each of you should take turns taking your child to the doctor and dentist. If you are the parent who receives your child's report card, copy it and send it to the other parent. Do this with medical and extracurricular activity information, such as your child's Little League schedule. Do not complain to the other parent when he or she is 10 minutes late for an exchange of your child, and don't argue over whose turn it is to get your child's next haircut. Have parameters in your parenting plan for some of these things and ignore the rest.

"When parents are trying to disengage, but communication is necessary, it is often best if non-emergency communication is done by mail, fax or email. Only use faxes if both of you have sufficient privacy where you will receive the fax. By putting your communication in writing, you will have time to gather your thoughts and make sure that the tone is not argumentative. This also lets the receiving parent take some time and gather his thoughts so that he is not impulsive or angry in his response. Sarcasm is never helpful when trying to disengage from conflicts. Don't share your emails and faxes with your children; they are simply meant to share important information between the parents. Try to limit non-emergency communication to twice a month, except for sharing information that is time-sensitive (like faxing a notice from school to the other parent on the day you receive it). Obviously, emergency information about illnesses and injuries, unforeseen delays in visitation (as a result of traffic conditions, for example), or immediate school concerns should be shared by phone as soon as possible. However, by reducing general communication, and by putting necessary communications in writing, you will go a long way toward disengaging from conflict."

Research shows that mediation works approximately 80 percent of the time. As such, it is a viable alternative when the ex-spouses are not able to negotiate and/or to help settle those issues that cannot be resolved by negotiation. When negotiation and mediation will not work, the couple can go to court. In this case, just as in negotiation and mediation, you will want to be incredibly well prepared and you must have a lawyer who will protect your interests. It is also helpful for any couple who does go to court to assess the transaction costs, both in terms of the amount of money going to court will cost and the further damage that going to court can do to the relationship between the ex-spouses. That said, sometimes going to court is the only option left and it may be the only option that will work.

10
Forgive Yourself and Your Ex-Spouse

Forgiveness is a way of reaching out from a bad past and heading out to a more positive future.

— Marie Balter

Negotiators need the wisdom to know if, when and how to forgive the other party for acts — both real and imagined — if progress is to be made. The issue of forgiveness arises when one party believes that he or she has been hurt, wronged, or betrayed by the other party. Some of the time there is no need for forgiveness because just by being able to communicate and listen to each other, it becomes clear that the problem developed through a misunderstanding or a mistaken assumption. In other cases where there has been hurt and the other party has been wronged and/or betrayed and in order for forgiveness to take place there are four primary conditions that have to be met:

1. An acknowledgement of the other party's perceptions and feelings.

2. An admission of guilt and a repudiation of what took place in the past.

3. A resolve that the situation not repeat itself.

4. An agreement on developing a future that will be different from the past.

Author Trudy Govier writes eloquently on the art of forgiveness in her piece, "The Ethics of Forgiveness," in the Fall 1994 issue of *Interaction*: "Many mediators and proponents of conflict resolution are loathe to make moral judgments about causes, a reticence which is commendable in many contexts. In understanding forgiveness, however, an attempt to avoid moral judgments can be misleading. Forgiveness emerges from a background of moral agreement about what constitutes an offense. The whole idea of forgiveness presupposes that one party has wronged another, and that the one who had done wrong admits it and repents, whereupon the other may forgive him. Forgiveness thus requires a victim, an offender or wrongdoer, and a common understanding that the offender has done something wrong."

An example from a BBC documentary film illustrates the liberating and transformational effects of forgiveness. In the documentary, a BBC journalist interviews a British army officer who had been savagely beaten as a POW by a Japanese officer while being held captive during the building of the bridge on the River Kwai. At the time the documentary was made, the British officer was in his late 70s and continued to suffer from post-traumatic stress related to his captivity and brutal treatment. When asked what he would do if he ever met the Japanese officer who beat him, he replied, "Kill him."

The BBC was able to locate the Japanese officer, who by this time had become a Buddhist monk, and arranged for the two men to meet. The two men were placed at opposite ends of the bridge over the River Kwai. As the film progresses, the two old men slowly start to walk toward each other. There is a great deal of suspense because no one knows what either one will do when they meet. They stop two feet in front of each other. The Japanese officer respectfully bows to the British officer. The British officer slowly moves his right hand up and shakes hands with his ex-tormentor. The Japanese officer says that God had brought them together, looks the British officer directly in the eye and asks for his forgiveness. In that moment, the two men were set free from the past.

Astute negotiators, mediators, and peacemakers understand the power of forgiveness and the power of an apology. The following example powerfully illustrates the power of forgiveness: When I was working as a psychologist, I had a client whose daughter was being treated for leukemia at the local children's hospital. The child had completed her course of chemotherapy. The treatment was considered successful and the child was leukemia-free. However, the treatment protocol called for the injection of one more shot of chemotherapy as a precautionary measure to make sure that all of the cancerous cells had been destroyed.

Tragically, there were a series of mistakes that occurred during this particular treatment and the chemotherapy shot was mistakenly injected into the child's spinal cord instead of into her bloodstream. By the time the mistake had been discovered, it was too late. The child would die, piece by piece, as the chemotherapy, which is a neurotoxin, proceeded up her spinal cord into her brain. This was an incredibly heartbreaking experience for everyone involved, including the doctors, nurses, and hospital administrators who could do nothing to help her. After she died, I continued to work with, and support, the parents.

One year after the child died, her mother asked if I would arrange a meeting between herself and the physician who had made the fatal mistake. I provided a meeting place and a supportive environment for two people who needed to say some very important and very painful things to each other. The result of that meeting was that there was at least a partial forgiveness and each of the participants had the ability to get on with their lives in a better way than they would have if the meeting had not taken place.

I have the utmost respect for the mother who asked for the meeting and for the physician who agreed to attend. The lessons learned were to have the courage to ask for painful meetings that we would rather not attend, to attend them anyway, to be courageous and assertive enough to say what needs to be said, and to give the other party the opportunity to hear what the situation looks like from our point of view while listening to what the situation looks like from the other party's point of view.

Forgiveness can take a lot of time and effort as Zachary's example points out.

> I negotiated my original divorce settlement during a time of buoyant entrepreneurial success. My business was booming and the result of that success found its way into a generous settlement. Five years later, the bottom fell out of my business. I lost everything. Everything, that is, but legal obligation to maintain a well-larded contract. The traumatic

upshot for me came by way of the ex's swift retaliation when I could no longer keep up the big support payments. She said, "Say goodbye to your son, Chump! You won't see him again!" And I haven't. Needless to say while the courts were adamantly meticulous about the financial calculus of divorce, they were languidly noncommittal, hemming and hawing about the breaches of visitation. The finance was quantifiable, the visitations just added up to an ambiguous, unmanageable war of he said, she said. This is why I'm now negotiating, post-divorce — way, way, post-divorce — a reduced cash settlement to cover my outstanding debt. My baby son is now 24. Remarkably, some of my outstanding support payments accumulated in years where my son's net income exceeded mine!

Bizarre as that sounds, I'm now looking for a well-intended, peaceful closure, probably because I'm war-weary. The cumulative punishment of years of post-divorce battle has finally tuckered me out, brought me to the door under the sign "forgiveness."

Not enough attention is paid to post-divorce. Divorce, after all, lasts forever; the problems, hang-ups, hassles, circumstances and such, all evolve. The state of divorce is dynamic, changing over time, as kids grow up, financial positions wax and wane, and new partners enter the scene. No one believes that the state of matrimony is static over time — couples evolve — so why is divorce generally seen as a monolith, like an unmoving tombstone? That's not the reality.

I'll soon be negotiating with my ex after more than 12 years of intense bickering, with each of us pointing at the other's so-called breaches to the original agreement. My goal is to change the state of my divorce, to conciliate, forgive, and I hope, focus on the positive. By contrast, and relatively speaking, setting up the divorce way back when it happened was a piece of cake. We both rushed through it just to get it over with as quickly as possible. Figuratively speaking, a divorce leaves a wake behind it lasting years and years, but also, in another sense it is a wake for a dead marriage. Most authorial attention bears exclusively the coping with divorce as dead marriage, neglecting this other key aspect of its living wake: the long-lasting repercussions, the painfully long aftermaths.

Exercise 32
Forgiveness

Have you had or witnessed an experience pertaining to forgiveness? In the space below, briefly describe the incident and write down what you learned.

Is there a situation where forgiveness could cause a breakthrough in your negotiations with your ex-spouse?

1. You Have to Forgive Yourself

Often we need to truly forgive ourselves before we can forgive others. Let me give a non-divorce example first and then we will look at a divorce example.

As a psychologist, I had a client who had been the victim of an acquaintance rape in 1976. Although 20 years had passed, she still felt very guilty about this incident and felt that it was having an effect on her marriage. The client agreed intellectually that her guilt was counterproductive, but it continued nonetheless. As part of the treatment I suggested that if she were comfortable we could develop a healing ritual to help her forgive herself. The ritual I suggested was that she carry 76 dollar coins around with her everywhere she went. The coins (representing the year in which she was raped) would serve as a constant reminder of her guilt. When she felt she was ready, she could donate the coins to a charity of her choice. After six days of lugging the coins around she donated them to charity. A week later she reported that the weight of the money was a constant reminder that she was making herself feel guilty and that it was a relief to give the money away. Follow-up three months later revealed that the issue of her guilt had been resolved.

The following story illustrates the importance of self-forgiveness in a separating couple.

> My marriage hadn't been good for years. It seemed like we had the same fight over and over again but had unofficially decided to stay together until the children had finished high school. My wife said I was emotionally unavailable and never talked to her about my feelings or asked her about hers. I experienced my wife as overly controlling; we could do anything we wanted to do as long as it was her

idea and we did it her way. As you can imagine, our sex life was nonexistent.

My wife had me convinced that I was emotionally cold, until I met a new coworker who had recently separated from her husband. We became close friends and eventually confidants and lovers.

Unfortunately, my wife became suspicious and one day had her suspicions confirmed when she read some of my email on my laptop computer. Although I never intended to hurt her or have an affair, I wanted to find out if I was capable of having a relationship. My wife, now my ex-wife, has never forgiven me and I suspect she will hold it over my head forever. What I can't understand is why she had to tell our children. At first my son Patrick wouldn't even talk to me, and our daughter Clair gave me the cold shoulder for months.

In truth, I don't think I could have gotten out of the marriage without having the affair or without waiting until the children had moved out of the house. It took me several years to forgive myself. At this point the children have forgiven me and I think they also see how controlling their mother can be. The point is, I had to forgive myself so I could move on with my life, with my new relationship, and with my relationships with my children.

2. You Have to Forgive Others

Often you have to forgive the other person so you can get on with your life, even if they have not admitted their mistake or apologized for their actions as Briana's story points out:

I had never known my husband, now my ex-husband, to be a vindictive person until after we separated. What made me crazy was that he tried to turn our children, our family, our friends, and neighbors against me by telling them things about me that were blatantly untrue. [What] was most hurtful, was that some of them started believing him.

I felt that I was in a real double bind. I could tell them all the things that would make Rick look bad, but if I did that I would be stooping to his level. If I didn't say anything, he would get away with assassinating my character.

Then I just decided one day that this had to stop at least as far as I was concerned. I wrote a brief letter to everyone involved, except our children, whom I told in person. In the letter and in the conversation with my children, I told them that I would not impugn Rick's character and that if he tried to impugn my character, they could chose to either believe it or not believe it and that I was going to live and enjoy my new life fully.

Rick never apologized, but his attacks diminished. Also because his attacks were so biased and vindictive, he lost a great deal of credibility with everyone. Amazingly, some of the friends that I had thought I had lost forever came back.

3. Develop a Forgiveness Action Plan

Developing a forgiveness plan is the best way to bring your intentions to fruition. The first step is to write down what you want to forgive yourself and/or your ex-spouse for, and write out a plan to accomplish this. For example, you may have to confront your ex-spouse about an issue that is still unresolved for you, you might want to write a letter to your ex-spouse and then keep it for a week or more before deciding whether or not it is in your best interest to send it, or you may need to ask for help from a friend or a professional counselor. In the end, you will have more energy for those things that are truly important by forgiving yourself and/or your ex-spouse.

This is not to say that all behavior is to be tolerated, accepted or forgiven. Any behavior that results in violence, unwanted sexual behavior, or behavior that puts a child's mental or physical health in danger is not to be tolerated. For example, Kara stated that:

> My husband Tony just came unglued after we separated. I was totally shocked because before the separation he always had such a high need to be in control. I then began to notice that when I came to pick the children up, he was slurring his words a bit. As time went on, I was convinced that he was drinking. One day I noticed that the front end of his car was bashed in. He said that someone had backed into him. However, on the way home, our children said that their Dad had rear-ended the car in front of him. When I confronted Tony about my fear that he was drinking and more importantly if he were drinking and driving, he could endanger his own, our children's, and/or

Exercise 33
Forgiveness Plans

List three areas where you need to forgive yourself and then list your plan for doing so.

1.

2.

3.

Plan:

List three areas where you need to forgive your ex-spouse and list your plan for doing so.

1.

2.

3.

Plan:

someone else's life — Tony told me to mind my own G-D business.

I knew I had to do something about this situation. I contacted Alcoholics Anonymous and I contacted my lawyer. We went to court and the judge modified our parenting agreement so that my ex-husband could not drive with the children in the car. Tony told me he was mad as hell and would never forgive me for what I had done. Although I found this whole episode terribly upsetting, with the help of Alcoholics Anonymous and my lawyer I knew that I had done the right thing because the safety of my children comes first.

Knowing when to and how to forgive yourself and your ex-spouse is integral to being able to negotiate with each other and to get on with your life. Knowing when to and how to forgive yourself and/or your ex-spouse is also one of the most important lessons you can teach your children. This raises an important question: Is forgiving the person who has hurt us always possible? The answer is no. But you can forgive yourself and move on. Forgiving yourself involves realizing and accepting that you made the best decision you were capable of making at the time. Anne Shirley, the protagonist from the beloved book *Anne of Green Gables,* said that each day starts out as a new day with no mistakes in it. And although none of us can change the past, we can change the future, and one of the best ways to do that is deciding — at the deepest level possible — to live as full and complete a life as possible.

Therapist Yvonne Dolan has devoted her life to helping people overcome sexual abuse. Although all forms of sexual abuse involve a betrayal of trust, one of the types of sexual abuse that is most difficult to overcome is having been sexually abused by one's parent. Yvonne, who had herself been sexually abused, states that one of the best forms of revenge is "living a full and complete life." This important lesson is also true for people who have gone through or are going through a divorce or separation; at some point we have to give ourselves permission to move forward.

One of the techniques that Yvonne Dolan has developed to help her clients move forward is "the letter to the future." You write the letter to the future by imaging your life at a certain time in the future, for example, ten years in the future. Then write as clearly and specifically as possible about your new imagined life from the time you get up in the morning until the time you go to bed at night. Write about what you are doing at work and write about your personal life.

A slight modification of this technique is to write two letters. In the first letter write about how your life turned out if you did not forgive your ex-spouse. In the second letter, write about how your life turned out as if you did forgive your ex-spouse. Then compare the letters and see if the information in the letters gives you any additional information about whether or not you should forgive your ex-spouse or not forgive your ex-spouse. An example of writing the two letters follow, but first I would like to give some background.

> Phyllis and Ken fell in love and married during their last year of university. Ken was accepted into a prestigious medical school on scholarships, but there still wasn't enough money to make ends meet, so Phyllis worked two jobs. When Ken was doing his residency there still wasn't enough money so Phyllis continued to work two jobs and time was even more scarce then money so they saw each other for small snippets of time here and there. Before Ken finished his residency, he told Phyllis that he had a big surprise. He was accepted to specialize in psychiatry at a prestigious university on the west coast. Everything about the move was left to Phyllis and she was getting more

and more discouraged about their marriage. She wanted to go on to graduate school and specialize in occupational therapy, but Ken thought it best if she continued to work for a year or two more before they started having children.

A year into his specialization, Ken told Phyllis that he had fallen in love with a woman who was also studying to be a psychiatrist. He said that he and Phyllis no longer had anything in common and that he needed a partner that was more of his intellectual equal. Phyllis thought they could work things out and asked Ken to go for marriage counseling. Ken declined saying that if anyone found out it could hurt his professional reputation. At this time, Phyllis wrote her two letters to the future, the first with a negative ending and the second with a positive ending. Both letters follow in Samples 8 and 9.

Writing two letters to the future will help you explore different scenarios. They also, especially the positive letter, give you some feed-forward. Feed-forward is often existential messages we give ourselves about how we should live our lives.

4. Follow-Up Conversations

My daughter is now 19 years old and is in second year at the University of Guelph. I was doing some work in Ontario and was able to visit her after I completed my work. I arrived in Guelph and we set off to find

Sample 8
First Letter to the Future: Negative

January 20, 2020

It has been ten years since we divorced. Ken is now a well established psychiatrist and writes a weekly column on how to have a good marriage. The @#@@!, @#@@!, @#@@! even uses his marriage as an example of excellence in his columns. They have two lovely children and I have none.

I have dated a few times but nothing ever came of it. I wanted desperately to go back to school but never seemed to be able to afford it. I still blame Ken for taking advantage of me and ruining my life. Worst of all, I never had the children or family of my own that I so desperately wanted.

Sample 9
Second Letter to the Future: Positive

January 20, 2020

It has been ten years since we divorced. Although Ken is well established in his career, I do not begrudge him his success. He worked hard and although I think he really did take advantage of me, in the end I pursued my dreams. I shared a house with four of my friends, continued to work two jobs, and earned my degree in occupational therapy.

I love my career and five years after I graduated I had the opportunity to work on a military base in Germany. It was a close call. The adventure of working in a foreign country was very appealing, but it was with severely injured military personnel who were maimed by landmines in Afghanistan. This type of work looked like it would be very difficult and I was very happy in my community and still shared a house with my four friends and was dating occasionally. Overall I was very happy and content. In the end I decided to go to Germany; it was a close call as 51 percent of me wanted to go and 49 percent of me wanted to stay.

In Germany I met my future husband. He was severely disabled and had burns to 40 percent of his body. I had never met anyone who was so determined to get better. He was an inspiration to everyone. Every once and a while I think of writing a thank-you note to Ken.

a restaurant. We were having a somewhat typical father and daughter conversation when our conversation turned to the subject of Katie's mother's and my divorce. At the end of our conversation, Katie told me that she would not have changed anything about the divorce. You could have knocked me over with a feather and the sense of relief that was flowing through my body was palpable. My son is away for a year travelling, but when he comes home, I am going to ask him the same question. As a psychologist, I find it interesting that sometimes we can be uptight about something and not even realize it. I was also very pleased that Katie felt that she could be that open with me and I look forward to future conversations at the same level of depth when they occur.

Sometimes we need professional help to move forward. Professional help is not a sign of weakness. It is a way to help you take control of your life, and this is the topic to which we turn our attention to next.

Exercise 34
Follow-up

Is there anyone that you could talk to and benefit from a follow-up conversation about your divorce/separation? What do you want to ask them?

5. When Professional Help Helps

You know you have forgiven yourself and your ex-spouse when you allow yourself to start over. Sometimes starting over requires professional help as Sarah's story points out.

My ex-husband became physically abusive four years into our marriage. By that time I had stopped working and had two young children to look after. I became more ashamed, and more depressed. We had a storybook romance and a storybook wedding. Every time it happened, Colin would apologize and I desperately wanted to believe him. Then one day, my four-year-old asked me why Daddy hit Mommy. Although I could take the abuse for myself, I couldn't let my children grow up thinking that this was a normal way to behave. My son's innocent question drove me to do something about the situation. I told my parents and my best friend. Both offered to take me and the children in. I decided to move in with my best friend until I could get my own place and start to live a new life. I also got counseling and I got stronger. Colin promised to get counseling too, but this was just another broken promise.

At first I couldn't forgive Colin for ruining my life, but in the end I met Patrick, a very nice guy, through an Internet dating site. I was very reluctant to get involved with anyone again, especially since he was starting to get serious much sooner than I could handle. I broke off the relationship and we remained friends for almost two years. Finally, Patrick told me he loved me too much to settle for being best friends. By this time I realized that I loved him too and was ready to have a real relationship.

During this transition I felt very vulnerable and it had nothing to do with Patrick. It was just a hangover from my relationship with my ex-husband. I went back to see my counselor and she helped me to accept Patrick's love, not just intellectually, but also emotionally. Part of my healing was to realize that for whatever reason, Colin was unable to change his behavior but that didn't mean that I couldn't change mine.

Exercise 35
Professional Help

What types of professionals have you used to help yourself in the past, e.g., doctors, lawyers, physiotherapists, etc.?

What type of person and/or professional could help you forgive either your ex-spouse and/or yourself in order to move on with your life and live a life that is as happy and productive as possible?

What criteria could help you decide if it was in your best interest to forgive or not?

Knowing when to, when not to, and how to forgive yourself and/or your ex-spouse is essential to living a full and complete life. A famous quote sometimes attributed to Ralph Waldo Emerson goes along the lines of, "One minute of anger robs you of 60 seconds of happiness." It is also often true that when we are miserable about a real or imagined hurt, the other person is oblivious or is not even thinking about it. So in the end, it looks like Yvonne Dolan is right: The best form of revenge is living a full and complete life.

Conclusion

I would like to end this book with a story that appeared in *The Buffalo News*.

In 1999, eleven-year-old Kevin Stephan's heart stopped beating after a baseball bat struck him in the chest. An off-duty nurse named Penny Brown performed CPR and saved his life.

When Kevin was 17, he saved a woman's life by administering the Heimlich maneuver as she choked on her lunch. "Kevin's mother — who happened to be in the restaurant that afternoon — was the first to realize the link between the two events … You saved my son's life seven years ago, and now he's saved yours."("Explorer youth saves life of woman who saved him years earlier," by Gene Warner; buffalonews. com, Feb 5, 2006.)

What can we learn from this story? Although our actions may not always come back to us, we can be certain that sometimes they will. It is also true that we do not possess the foresight to know when they will and when they will not. Therefore, a more prudent question to ask ourselves is, "Will we be happy with what we are doing today, when and if it comes back to us tomorrow?"

By learning how to negotiate more effectively, it will not only be better for the ex-spouses, it will also be better for their children. Even though your ex-spouse may not be your friend for the rest of your life, you will both always be your children's parents for the rest of your lives.

There will also be future events such as high school and/or university graduations, your children getting married and having children (your grandchildren), or there will be illnesses or possible tragic events, and at these times you both will want to be there physically, emotionally, and spiritually for your children. You don't want to have unresolved conflicts or a damaged relationship take away from your enjoyment of future celebrations or take away from your ability to cope effectively with difficult issues or situations that may arise. An example of how a couple's past difficulties in negotiating may negatively affect their ability to negotiate in the future follows in this story of Bruce, Laurie, Phillip, and Cassandra.

> Laurie and I had been married for 15 and a half years and have two children: Phillip, 12, and Cassandra, 9. We had been high-school sweethearts. My ex-wife remarried a year after we divorced.
>
> At first, we had joint custody and hers was the primary residence. She worked evenings so this worked out reasonably well. In fact, I had the children more than half of the time, because Laurie and her new husband led quite an active social life.
>
> Then something quite unexpected happened. I was offered an amazing job in a neighboring state. It was too good an opportunity to pass up, but we had never considered that either of us would move when we worked out separation and divorce agreements.
>
> At first Laurie was totally opposed to the idea of my moving. In the end, she agreed that I could move and that it would be in the children's best interest to have their primary residence with me. The verbal agreement also included the fact that she would have liberal phone access to the children and would see them once a month. As Laurie's parents lived approximately halfway between us, I would drive the children as far as Laurie's parents' and she would pick them up there, and we would reverse the procedure on their return to me. We had also agreed that Laurie would have the children for the first half of the summer and I would have them for the second half.
>
> We were in the process of writing up the agreement. I had moved to the new city and registered the children for school. School would begin in one week's time and the children were prepared psychologically for the move. We

were all starting to settle in when the bombshell dropped. Laurie called and said that she couldn't go through with it. The children were very confused. She told them she would take me to court, sue me for kidnapping, and go to the police. I was a basket case. In the end she agreed to allow the children to move, but the way she did it made it extremely difficult for all of us — herself included.

I was so worried and upset about how all of this would affect the children that I took them to see a psychologist. Sometimes they saw the psychologist together and sometimes separately. I asked the psychologist to help the kids deal with the kinds of stresses they get put under, and said that my interest was not to use anything from the sessions legally, and I certainly hoped it won't come to that.

At the present time, the children have not seen their mother for four months and my son has no interest in going to see her. However, I told him that Laurie is his mother and that he had to see her. Unfortunately, Laurie is now working on our daughter and telling Cassandra that she should live with her. The psychologist sent a letter to Laurie asking her to fill out a set of forms to help the psychologist treat the children, but Laurie wouldn't fill the forms out. Laurie did, however, send a letter to the psychologist that stated that she didn't think that anyone would be traumatized by splitting up the children. Even my ex-wife's lawyer has told her not to discuss custody and access directly with the children as this puts them squarely in the middle of what should be adult, and not the children's problems.

Unfortunately, everyone in this family is being affected negatively by the way Bruce and Laurie negotiate. Although counseling for the children may help, it might be more helpful if the family as a whole, and sometimes the different parts thereof could see a counselor or therapist who could help them negotiate in a healthier manner. If that is not possible, then Bruce should continue to get help for the children, but he should also consider getting some help for himself.

Bruce and Laurie also need to realize that there will be other major negotiations that will have to take place in the future. As children approach and then enter adolescence, negotiations and decisions will get more difficult. The negotiations will be difficult enough on their own, without introducing problems that could have and should have been sorted out in the past.

But this doesn't have to be the case. I attended the closing banquet for a group of young student leaders in science called Shad Valley. I was thoroughly impressed with this dedicated group of young high-school students who had been chosen to participate in this university-level program during the summer. At the banquet I meet a couple. I assumed they were married, until they said that they were divorced and had come to see their son graduate from the program. We had a long discussion over dinner and I was so happy to see that they had resolved all of the issues between them and could be fully present to enjoy the moment, their son's accomplishment, and being their son's parents. The relationship these parents had with their son and with each other is a testament to the importance of treating each other well and working cooperatively. Divorcing or separating individuals have a very important choice to make, and that choice is whether to make the divorce and post-divorce experience as positive as possible for every-one concerned.

The choice, ultimately, is up to you.

It is my hope that as the years pass, all of the stigma that has been unfairly attributed to divorcing and separating couples will dissipate to the point where we are as enlightened and supportive as we are for people who are having to deal with other major life transitions. Separating and divorcing, especially where there are children involved, is difficult enough without the parties having to defend their very per-sonal decisions to others and to society at large. It is also my hope, that the experiences of the people I interviewed, who so courageously shared their stories will inspire you to create your own innovative solu-tions and to have the flexibility, determination, and maturity to bring those solutions to fruition.

In your endeavors to apply these strategies and to build your fami-lies with creative rather than wasteful solutions, I wish you the best.

If you have any questions you would like to see addressed in future editions of this book, or if you have comments, or stories that would help readers, please contact me at brad@bradmcrae.com, and be as-sured that all identifying information will be eliminated.

Download Kit

Please enter the URL you see in the box below into your computer web browser to access and download the kit.

www.self-counsel.com/updates/negotiating/15kit.htm

The download kit offers forms in MS Word and/or PDF format so you can edit as needed. It includes:

- Samples and exercises to help you sharpen your negotiation skills
- Resources for further reading and viewing

OTHER TITLES OF INTEREST FROM SELF-COUNSEL PRESS

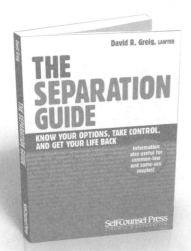

The Separation Guide:
Know Your Options, Take Control, and Get Your Life Back
David Greig, BA, LLB
ISBN 978-1-77040-057-3
6 x 9 • paper • 168 pp.
First Edition
$18.95 USD/$19.95 CAD

The Separation Guide: Know Your Options, Take Control, and Get Your Life Back is one of the most comprehensive guides for separation and divorce management available today. It is filled with practical and money-saving steps for dealing with assets, finances, legal processes, and even post-separation life planning.

Author and lawyer David Greig offers advice for all types of couples. including common-law and same sex couples.

Readers in relationships headed for or in a separation phase need to know:

- When it is over so they can plan ahead.
- How to understand their legal case.
- Why a separation agreement may be a good idea.
- How to manage finances, assets, and liabilities including pets, pensions, and possessions.

Whether the outcome is separation, divorce, or staying together, *The Separation Guide* will help individuals to understand their case, know their options, take control and get their lives back in track.

The Author

Author and lawyer David Greig is a practicing family and divorce lawyer. He is the author of *Separation Agreement*, another Self-Counsel Press title.